From a Fishhook to an Ax...
Learn How to Sharpen Like a Pro!

Hunters, fishermen, hikers, campers, homemakers, do-it-yourselfers—here at last is the book you've always wanted but could never find. John Juranitch shows even the lowest ranked beginner how to put the sharpest edge on the dullest tool, and also restore old tools for years of trouble-free service and wear. Everything you need to know is here:

The basic theory of sharpening

Safe knife handling and use

Handling a hone

The best angle to sharpen at

How to buy a knife—and kiss the gimmicks good-bye

What to look for when buying hones

Carbon steel versus stainless: finally, the real winner!

How to tell if your knife is sharp

Serrated edges: how good are they? For what?

Sharpening the most popular blades in use today: including scissors, knives, axes, chain saws, adzes, folding knives, and plane blades —specific techniques, detailed "how-to" photographs and precise drawings

How to build your own hollow grinder— instructions within!

Step-by-step lessons featuring over 100 photographs and diagrams for ease and accuracy—and much more!

MEET THE PRO: John Juranitch has been a professional sharpening consultant since 1951, numbering among his clients Country Pride, Oscar Meyer, Swift & Co., Northern Seas, and others throughout the midwest and Canada. For his company, Razor Edge Systems, Inc., he makes frequent appearances at annual sportsmen's conventions and on television demonstrating the remarkable feat of sharpening and shaving with a double-bitted ax—a show-stopping accomplishment for which Juranitch holds the Guinness World Record (14 minutes).

THE RAZOR EDGE BOOK OF SHARPENING

John Juranitch

with Rose Juranitch, Joe Juranitch, Randy Meskill, and Mary Meskill

WARNER BOOKS

A Warner Communications Company

Copyright © 1985 by John Juranitch
All rights reserved.
Warner Books, Inc., 666 Fifth Avenue, New York, NY 10103

W A Warner Communications Company

Printed in the United States of America
First printing: March 1985
10 9 8 7 6 5 4

Library of Congress Cataloging in Publication Data

Juranitch, John.
  The razor edge book of sharpening.

  1. Sharpening of tools.   I. Title.
TJ1280.J817 1985   621.9′3′0288   84-3641
ISBN 0-446-38002-4 (U.S.A.) (pbk.)
      0-446-38003-2 (Canada) (pbk.)

Cover photograph of John Juranitch by Pam Roberts.
Photographs on pages 7–9 taken for the Ely Echo by Pam Roberts

Designed by Giorgetta Bell McRee

CONTENTS

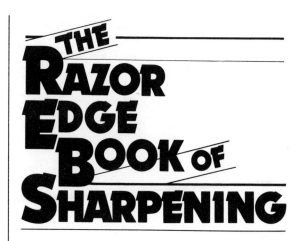

THE IMPORTANCE OF THE EDGE

Few people realize how important the edge is, not only to their everyday lives, but to mankind as a whole. In the dawn of man's existence, he basically did three things: he hunted, he fished, and he fought to stay alive. He accomplished all three of these things through the use of an edge, and his very survival was dependent on it. He had no sharp teeth, no claws, wasn't very strong, and was slower than the other beasts. However, he had one thing in his favor—the edge.

He first took a piece of rock, probably one already ideally shaped, and ground it against another rock, thereby producing an edge. He then attached this edge to a stick, enabling him to strike out with it, as with a spear or ax; with this weapon he more than made up for his weaknesses. With his edge man gained respect and ensured his survival.

So perhaps man's most important invention was not really the wheel, for if he had not invented the edge first, he would never have survived to invent the wheel. Before the advent of gunpowder, the blade ruled the world for many thousands of years in the hands of the legions of war. The edge was supreme.

Today, everything we touch in our daily lives has been formed in one way or another through the use of edges. The paper you are looking at was first a tree that had been cut down with an ax or saw. The by-products of that tree were then processed and cut to size many, many times before they became this book.

The fabrics in your home and the clothing you wear all had to pass through many processes involving the use of a cutting edge.

And the car you drive. All of its parts were either machined or punched out, using edges.

Yet in spite of its importance, very little is

known about the edge. Little has been written on the subject, and unfortunately, much of this has been filled with old wives' tales.

Strangely enough, man learned to walk on the moon before he learned to sharpen his knife properly. It's just a fact.

MEET YOUR AUTHORS

We would like you to have total confidence in us as authors of this book, so we are going to tell you something about us.

Our study of sharpening began in 1951, when as an Army barber, the straight razor and hone held a fascination for John Juranitch, who is founder and president of our company. There was nothing written on the subject at the time, and still isn't really, so he began his own study of the subject of sharpening, which eventually led to the formation of Razor Edge Systems, Inc.

Today we are responsible for setting up sharpening systems in some of the largest meat packing plants in the world. It is our job to solve any edge-related problem, regardless of its nature. Tests have shown that just by using extremely sharp edges production will increase by as much as 8 percent.

Now our work is taking us into other industries, such as the textile industry and the film industry, where poor edges are responsible for millions of dollars of waste.

The following pages will explain our ability to solve sharpening and edge problems, and even more important, our expertise in teaching others how to do it. Our world championships and records speak for themselves.

Presently we live in Ely, Minnesota, which is a small wilderness town on the Canadian border, and we are all owner-employees of Razor Edge Systems, Inc., which manufactures and distributes sharpening machinery, tools, and technology to industry as well as to the sportsman and home hobbyist.

This book is the result of many years of research, development, experimenting, and note taking. Just the other day, one of our boys said, "Dad, I can remember when I was about nine years old and you were working on this book." Well, that young boy is now almost a quarter century old and that book has just been completed. Had we realized at the time just how mammoth a project we were undertaking, perhaps we would never have gotten started. But we're glad we did, for these past years have been rewarding, and the knowledge we have gained is invaluable.

As you read through this book, it is our hope that something will awaken inside you, and that the material we have shared in these pages will instill in you some of the understanding and experience that has taken us over thirty years to acquire in this fascinating and rewarding field of edges.

Standing in front of the bathroom mirror and shaving with a knife got to become just sort of routine to us after a few years, and seemed as normal as using a safety razor. Then the thought dawned that it would make a good demonstration seeing someone pull out a dull hunting knife, sharpen it up, and shave his beard off with it. Well, the idea caught on at sports shows, and the media had a field day with it, too. It wasn't unusual to have every local television station show up whenever we pulled this stunt. At a show in Los Angeles we were guests on every station except one.

Later, to make our demonstration a little more spectacular, we came up with another idea: how about putting a little girl with a dull hunting knife up against a licensed master barber with a straight razor in a shaving contest? It sounded like a pretty good idea, so we tried it in Kansas City and it turned out to be a real crowd pleaser. All three judges gave the decision to the girls, and there was no doubt who the crowd was pulling for. Chances are that they would have tarred and feathered the judges had the decision come out any differently.

The following pictures are a practice session and were taken when the girls were eleven and twelve. It's easy to see why this event was such a crowd pleaser.

Picture 2 *Here are the girls with their victim. It's always a good idea to increase their allowance just before tricks like this. It's cheap but very good insurance. They are using skinning knives, usually considered one of the most difficult of all to sharpen. We'll see. You'll note that as shaving time draws closer, the look on the girls' faces gets a little more serious.*

Picture 1 *Here are Mary and JoAnn with their shaving mugs in one hand and their knives in the other. According to the rules of our contest, the girls must start out with a dull knife and then do their own sharpening. Note the smiles as we are just getting under way.*

Picture 3 *The girls are sharpening their weapons; notice we have both a right-handed and a left-handed "barber lady." The hone hand "feels" the edge all the way around the curve of the blade. The hone hand is constantly moving, as is the knife hand.*

Picture 4 *Mary wins the coin toss and chooses to start the shaving. Now you won't even detect the slightest hint of a smile on her face.*

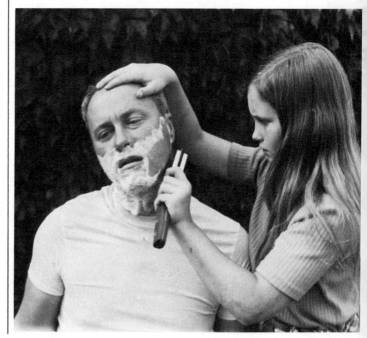

First the girls go to town with their mugs and brushes. They know this job will have a big influence on the outcome of their shave, so they aren't going to spare any shaving cream. Here Mary is into the most difficult part of the shave—under the chin and down the throat. Sure hope she's careful around that jugular.

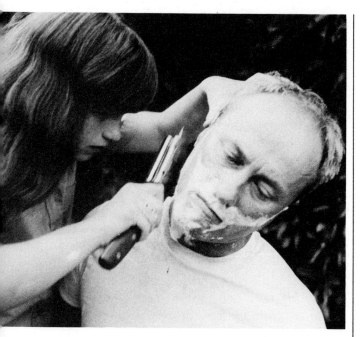

Picture 5 *Now it's JoAnn's turn and everything looks all business. You will notice that JoAnn likes to grasp the knife back on the handle, while Mary sneaks way up on the blade. Guess you have to use what works best for you!*

Picture 6 *After a few tense moments we finally have mission accomplished, and a shave as close as any barber's. You can see we are just beginning to get some of those smiles back that we saw earlier. Either they are glad to be done or they are thinking about how they will spend that extra allowance. If you didn't get the point of all this, here it is: if two little girls can sharpen a knife so that it will shave this well, why can't you? All you need is a little knowledge about the edge. Read on!*

THE PURPOSE OF THIS BOOK

We want to put to rest once and for all, all the gimmickry and old wives' tales concerning the sharpening of edges and give you the knowledge and understanding you need to produce the most unbelievable edges on any cutting tool.

First we will familiarize you with sharpening theory and related subjects by explaining some of our research and development projects and describing experiences we have had during the past thirty years of studying the edge.

Although some of our research and experimenting was done in the tanning industry, most of our information has come from the meat packing industry. This includes beef, pork, turkey, chicken, and fish plants. There are several reasons for this. First of all, by far the main use of a knife is in preparing food. For the sportsman this could mean anything from cleaning a deer to skinning a bear, filleting a fish, or dismembering a fowl. And this is what the packing industry is all about, only instead of small quantities as the average sportsman would be concerned with, they work with huge quantities. In some of the packing plants we have trained, there are thousands of head of cattle slaughtered and processed every day. In one fish plant they had over 180 people who specialized in one thing only, and that was filleting fish for eight hours a day.

There are many different people doing many different jobs in one plant. The variety and quantity of knives they use is considerable, and many plants have their own knife and blade designs for different jobs. As we have worked in various plants throughout the United States and Canada, we have encountered a multitude of knife and blade designs. Some were very good, and some were very bad. Multiply this by the number of packing plants there are and it is easy to un-

derstand that when it comes to edges, knives, or related subjects, the meat packing industry is where it is happening. And it is happening every day for long periods of time. It is not unusual to help a meat cutter who has been sharpening his own knife every day for thirty or forty years. In one plant we ran into a guy who had been sharpening his own knife for over sixty years! We have to give credit to the ladies, too. Many of these positions are filled by women who do a super job. They are particularly good in jobs requiring accuracy in cutting, and a good number of them can sharpen a knife a lot better than many men can.

As we go through some of our research with you, you will become familiar with edges. You will then have a good background and be ready for step-by-step lessons in sharpening some of the most commonly used edged tools. We'll start with the easiest and most common blades and go through the sharpening of each tool so that they are all clearly understood.

Remember, our primary objective is to enable you to get the ultimate edge on your very first try. Before starting on the first tool, be sure you completely understand everything you have read. Go over it if necessary, and keep going over it until you have a clear idea of what you must do, and also *why* you must do it.

YOU CAN DO IT!

How many times have we watched in awe as someone did something spectacular? As a youngster, maybe it was watching the Lone Ranger shoot a gun out of the villain's hand without even drawing blood. As an adult, perhaps it was Elvis Presley, Muhammad Ali, or maybe John Glenn as he traveled to outer space. We probably just said something to ourselves, like "Wow, I wish I could do that!" But it was a hopeless wish, one we knew was impossible. We felt we didn't have the patience to learn to do what we had seen, or perhaps we felt that we didn't have the talent.

What does all this mean? Simple. In the following pages we are going to show you something spectacular, so you'll say, "Wow, I wish I could do that." And then, perhaps for the first time in your life, instead of the hopelessness you've experienced before, you will be able to say, "I can do it!"

One of the most spectacular demonstrations of the edge is shaving with a butcher knife. Well, we went one further and shaved with a double-bitted ax. The following pictures were taken at the World's First Annual Ax Sharpening and Ax Shaving Contest.

WORLD CLASS AX SHARPENING AND AX SHAVING

Picture 7 *Bob Cary, well-known editor, writer, guide, and 1980 presidential candidate on the Independent Fisherman's Party, reads the rules of the contest and calls for any and all challengers to step forward, while Randy Meskill, author/editor and master of ceremonies, listens closely.*

Picture 8 *After the judges have made sure that the ax is good and dull, author/contestant John Juranitch begins sharpening his edge as he explains what he is doing and fields as many questions as possible.*

Picture 9 *John gives the ax a final inspection prior to the shaving contest. Next comes the shaving cream and a few prayers.*

Picture 10 *The TV cameras roll and so do the whiskers. Note the chunk of beard falling from the chin. The chin is a difficult area to shave, and if nicks are going to happen, this is the place.*

Picture 11 *The throat not only is a tender area; it also has vital arteries close to the surface of the skin, so John uses extreme caution. The people in the background have rather tense looks on their faces, while Randy seems calm . . . just another day's work!*

Picture 12 *John finally finishes and everyone breathes a sigh of relief. He still looks rather healthy and has a good, clean shave. He has also set the world record for both ax sharpening and ax shaving. Congratulations, John!*

PART 1 WHAT EVERYONE NEEDS TO KNOW ABOUT EDGES

CHAPTER 1

The Questions Most Asked About Sharpening

In this chapter we will answer some of the questions that we hear most often. They come from sportsmen, professionals, people we've met at sports shows and packing plants, and in letters from people like you. The answers to these questions will give you a good start in understanding what sharpening is all about, and perhaps you will find sharpening to be much easier than you ever thought it would be.

We do not claim to know everything there is to know about edges—in fact, we are still learning things that sometimes surprise us—but we are the only company in the world that specializes in the study of the edge. We have been involved in this study for over thirty years, and one of the most important lessons we have learned is that "it pays to listen."

In our early years of experimenting, things were very interesting, very rewarding, and something else—*hectic!* We could even underline that last one. There were several reasons for this, and certainly financial problems were among them. Another was the fact that we didn't really know what we were doing and had to rely on the opinions of others to grade our efforts.

Many times when we would go into a packing plant, the supervisor would give our edges to the top men in the plant to evaluate. Now here was another problem. You see, being a butcher is not just cutting meat. Being a butcher is sharpening the knife, and the ability to sharpen is what separates the good butchers from the poor ones. The best butchers in a plant are superb, but they are few and far between, 5 percent at the most. They have pride, they are looked up to, and they are something of a hero in the eyes of their fellow workers, and naturally they enjoy this. Being the best, they have a right to be proud. But then one day something happens to these men. A stranger walks into the plant and tells them he is going to sharpen their knife. They resist giving up their knife because they don't want anyone ruining it, and because they resent someone else's ability to sharpen. Then the real shock hits them. The new edge is better than theirs was, and now all of a sudden everyone is equal because they all have the same edges, and they are losing their status. So what do they do as a defense? They fight back by being as difficult as they can. You can't blame them. Who wouldn't? At first we didn't know what was going on. Why were these men nasty to us, when all we were doing was trying to help them? We should have been given the red carpet treatment for even trying to help them, but instead there was abuse, even though we made their day easier.

It took us quite a while before we caught on to this problem, and it became clear that solving the problems of the edge was only a part of our job. So what did we call this problem? Certainly it had to have a name, as it was going to become a part of our daily work. We decided on professional jealousy. Little did we know, but professional jealousy was going to follow us wherever we went.

Edge problems have led us into other industries, such as textiles, film, fiber, and surgical equipment. Wherever we went, our old friend professional jealousy was waiting for us. A film company asked us to come in to talk about the problems of slitting film. The film in your cassette is manufactured in huge, wide rolls, and is then slit into the thin, desired sizes. A battery of slitters is used, and sometimes something happens to the slitters that no one understands. The result is a considerable loss. Well, we did all right with the fellow who had sought our help, but that is where it ended. We met the man responsible for technology in this department, and it was clear that we would never get beyond the lobby. "My name is Doctor So and So, and do you know that I am an expert in sharpening?"

was his opening sentence. Clearly his goal was to get rid of us as quickly as possible; he obviously felt that we were a threat to his security. But he is still living with his slitting losses, needlessly.

We realize that everyone is not going to agree with everything we say in this book. But keep in mind we are stating what we have found and believe to be true as a result of our many years of intensive study. Each of our conclusions is based not on speculation or opinion, but on the results of numerous experiments and experiences.

If you find something you disagree with, by all means study it and do some testing on your own. You may be surprised at what you learn, and you may even end up finding yourself in total agreement with us.

WHAT KNIFE SHOULD I BUY?

We hear this question at every class we hold or whenever someone can corner us for a question. They ask us the question, and then with eager eyes and wide-open ears expect to hear the great revelation. We anticipate the letdown, so we cushion its shock as much as possible with a list of things to look for.

The quality of American-made knives is generally very good. Modern steels are excellent. You will be confronted by many claims by manufacturers concerning the merits of their knives, and particularly of the steels used in them. They all want you to think that they send a special rocket to the moon to pick up a load of special steel that is available only to them. This is good advertising. The fact of the matter is that no steel mill is going to run a special steel for someone like a knife manufacturer, who uses only small quantities. How would the manufacturer know what steel to order in the first place, and by what standard would he choose? There are no known methods of testing steels for their ability to either take or hold an edge, and doing this would require a tremendous background in edges, which is something a knife manufacturer simply does not have. They might be terrific at their profession of making knives, and many of them are, but edges are entirely another field.

If you are buying a knife, a good way to choose is to look all of them over and pick the one that most appeals to *you.* It's got to have eye appeal—*your* eye appeal. After all, you are the one buying it, and you are the one who is going to be using it.

One year while deer hunting, we ran across a young deer hunter who had found just the knife he wanted. Quite stylish, he had on a safari hat, a deer rifle slung over his shoulder, a big Western-style six-gun strapped to one leg, and a huge Bowie knife strapped to the other. Not really too practical for walking, especially not in our northern Minnesota woods, but that's not the point. That knife just plain did something for that young fellow—besides weighing him down!

Go to some store that has a large selection of knives, take a bunch out, and look 'em over real good. Place them side by side and notice the craftsmanship. Are edges nicely finished off, or are they uneven and rough? In the case of a folding knife, are the moving parts closely fitted, or are there spaces between them? Does the blade snap open and lock solidly, or is there a lot of play in the blade? One more big consideration is safety. If you can, get a blade that locks open. All you need is a blade folding over your knuckles while you're out on some wilderness hunt. These blade-locking knives are really becoming popular, and with good reason.

The choice between the sheath knife and the folding knife is, again, a personal one. There is little doubt that the guy with the sheath knife has a little more of the macho image going for him, sort of like Daniel Boone or Jim Bowie. Like the guy we saw with the big knife strapped to his leg.

There is another thing you'll want to consider: a knife spends most of its time just being carried around, either in a pocket or on a belt. So this brings out another concern, that of comfort. Regardless of how you carry your knife, if it's not comfortable, you are not going to be carrying it around for very long. If it pokes you in the belly or feels like a railroad spike in your pocket, you will soon be more content with comfort than with the knife. Then it will end up in the back of your "I never use it" drawer. And if it ends up there, you would have been better off saving your money in the first place, because a knife in the drawer does you no good.

If you're considering a folding knife, stick it in your pocket and see if it's comfortable there. (But don't let it get so comfortable that you walk out the door with it!) If it's too heavy, too bulky, or too square, you will not be comfortable with it.

If your choice is a sheath knife, put it on and walk around with it. Sit in a chair, and in a car seat, too. Now how does it feel? If you find it uncomfortable, try a folding knife on the belt. It might be a little less macho, but it could be your answer. Remember, all you need in a blade is a few inches, and anything over that is purely imagination. Unless, of course, you are hunting dinosaur, in which case you'll need a Bowie like our young hunter friend had.

If you live in the desert, you probably won't be interested in the type of steel your knife is made of, but if you live elsewhere, listen closely. Consider stainless. If you happen to leave your knife in a wet pair of pants and forget about it, you won't be greeted with a worthless piece of rust a couple of weeks later. This will be covered further in the next question.

The handle is the most neglected part of many a knife. For the sportsman it is not as critical as to the professional, but it's important nonetheless. The handle is to the knife as the steering wheel is to the automobile. It should enable you to guide it quickly, effortlessly, and most important, *surely,* in the direction you want it to go. And that *surely* is more important than you might think.

Consider the average sportsman as he uses his knife. He has just downed the buck he has been dreaming about all year long, and is very excited. His hands are probably cold, maybe wet, or even greasy. Chances of an accident happening are good. Let's look at several knife handle designs and consider their merits.

In Figure 1-1 we can see that knife A has a straight handle and is often squared on both sides, as indicated by lines 1 and 2. We call this a "broom handle," and it just isn't the greatest. It has nothing that fits the contour of your hand or fingers, and it has no guard to prevent your hand from slipping up on the blade. This is a very poor design for a handle.

Knife B has the worst design for a handle we have ever seen; unfortunately there are a lot of these knives around. This handle is usually round and it lacks a guard, allowing your fingers to get up on the blade. To make it even worse, it tapers toward the blade. The width at 1 is greater than the width at 2, and this increases the chances of an accident called stubbing, which is responsible for a good many nasty cuts.

Let's explain stubbing. Stubbing usually occurs when you move a knife toward something, but you do not clear obstacles. Let's say you have a chunk of meat on the table and you are going to do some trimming. You get your knife, walk over to the table, and while you are bring-ing your knife out over your work to do your cutting, you do not clear the edge of the table. You are used to bringing just your hand over the table without anything in it. But now you have something protruding six inches or so from your hand, and you don't allow for it. It's awkward and clumsy. Instead of clearing the table, your knife tip sticks into it and stops, allowing your hand, which at this moment is very loosely grasping the handle, to slide up on the blade. It may not always be a table. This could happen while reaching inside a deer to remove some tissue. In any case, the results are obvious.

Knife C has a type of guard that is commonly used and works well. Notice that the taper of the handle at point 1 is greater than at point 2, so the handle is easier to hang on to.

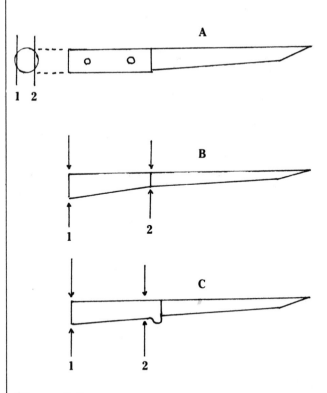

Figure 1-1

In some packing plants, they insist on large guards that prevent stubbing, and they won't accept a knife that has the guard altered. Some guards are made of metal and are so big we have a hard time getting them in our sharpening machine. But all you have to do is have one encounter with stubbing, as many butchers have, and from then on all your knives will have a guard of some kind or another.

IS STAINLESS STEEL ANY GOOD FOR KNIVES?

For some reason, stainless steel has picked up a bad reputation. Maybe grandma's first stainless steel butter knives just weren't that great, we don't really know. We had heard the complaint enough, though, so it was time to start digging into the subject to see what the real truth is.

We were experimenting in a large beef packing plant that slaughtered close to a thousand head a day. The training of the men on the lines was pretty well behind us, so we had some time for study. This company was using a well-known brand of knife, and while sharpening some of the blades we noticed that many of these knives were identical, with the exception that some were high carbon and some were stainless steel. We had noticed this in other plants, and it gave us the idea of testing one against the other. We all agreed that this would be an interesting study, so we chose two brand-new knives identical in every respect except for one being high carbon and one stainless steel.

We took the two knives over to the machine, sharpened them identically, and tested the edges to make sure they were exactly the same. They were as equal as it was humanly possible to get them, so our next step was to find someone to do the testing. The foreman pointed out his two best and most reliable butchers. Both had been there many years and they were doing different jobs. After talking it over, we decided not to tell them what we were looking for so that they would not favor one knife over the other.

We approached the first man, asked him to use the knives as equally as possible, and see if he had a preference between the two, or if he could tell any difference between them. We all went back to our work and about an hour later walked over to this butcher and asked how he was doing. "Notice any difference in the knives?" we asked. We got a simple "Nope."

We waited another hour before returning to the employee and asked, "How's it going?" He hesitated, looked at his edge, and said, "Well, this one seems to be dying. Don't know why." We looked at the knife, and it was the high carbon steel. "How is the other knife?" we asked. "Oh, good" was his short answer. He started to notice a difference and things were getting interesting, so now we were going to check every half hour.

So we dropped back in a half hour and asked how he was doing. "Good," he said, "but that one knife gave out." We took the knife from him, looked it over, and sure enough it was dull. It was the high carbon steel. "Well, then, what's the other knife like?" We looked it over and it was just as he said it was—excellent. We handed the knife back, told him to continue using it, and we would keep checking on it. We went back every half hour to check the knife, and things were always "Good."

At the end of the day, we caught the man on the way to the locker room and asked how he liked that knife. "Good! I'm going to use it tomorrow, too," he said. This was very surprising because it was contrary to everything we had always heard.

The next day we ran another test, using two

different knives and also a different employee. Results? Pretty much the same. The stainless knife outlasted the high carbon by better than four times, and it was still going.

Our next experiment on this subject was in a poultry plant on the East Coast, and we worked the test in much the same way. The person we chose for the test was a woman who had been there a long time and was the top knife person in the plant. She also had a great sense of humor and was always good for a laugh, so this experiment was more fun for us. This lady's name was Mary, but the Southerners pronounced it "Murry." Anyhow, Mary's job was different, because she cut almost all bone. It was her job to remove the breast of the chicken from the backbone, a very fast job. Those chickens just seemed to come flying down the conveyor chain.

We handed Mary the two identical-looking knives, didn't indicate what we were looking for, and just told her to use them equally. Results? Just about the same as for the beef plant. There was just no comparison between the high carbon and the stainless steel blades. We have run other such tests, and have always found the same answer. Stainless over high carbon by a wide margin.

The knife and the wrench in Picture 1-1 were both lost in some hay in our barn, and then ended up in the manure pile. We don't know which got there first, but both were probably there for about a year. The wrench we cleaned off and soaked in a pail of oil, to no avail. It was a total loss. The knife, however, is stainless, and a little water made it like new. If the knife had been of high carbon, like the wrench, it would also have been a total loss.

Just one more thought on steel. So many times you hear an ad offering a knife made of "surgical steel." Don't be impressed by this. Just go through the yellow pages and call a few warehouses that supply special steels to industry. Tell them you are interested in some surgical steel, and ask for price and delivery. Surprise! You will hear laughter and then be informed that there is no such animal.

We have been involved in the study of surgical tools, scalpels being one of them. They are made out of stainless steel as well as high carbon steel. Once, while in a meeting with the largest manufacturer of scalpels in the world, just to see what he would say, we asked the man in charge of manufacturing, "Mike, what is surgical steel?" He looked dumbfounded, shrugged his shoulders, and said, "I don't know!"

Next time you're in the local supermarket, notice the displays near the cash register. You'll see plenty of razor blades, and strangely enough, most of them seem to be stainless steel. Just for the heck of it, why don't you run your own test? The next time you buy razor blades, get a pack of stainless and a pack of high carbon. Get two holders and use them equally. Treat them the same, and store them the same. Remember that you are not cutting meat (hopefully, anyhow),

Picture 1-1

but are cutting whiskers. Chances are you'll learn something from your test, with one blade stainless, the other high carbon steel.

HOW DO I SHARPEN THE TEETH ON MY KNIFE?

You are not supposed to have any teeth on your knife! Sure, every article you have read on sharpening tells you in as many words as possible about the "microscopic teeth" on your edge and how they cut. It seems that writers are always trying to outdo one another, and pretty soon you have so many old wives' tales back to back that all you end up with is a wild story. Even professional cutlery manufacturers, who should know better, claim the same thing.

Well, we have to confess that when we were just getting started, we thought the same thing. That's why we "sawed" with our knife, as if we were cutting timber or something. It only made sense, because everything we had ever read on sharpening told us about these little teeth on our edge. As we got into our research, though, that idea of teeth turned into nonsense. We were running into a lot of questions that did not add up. Why were the dull edges the only ones you could feel these so-called teeth on? When the edge really cut slick, why did it feel smooth? How come you don't have to "saw" the whiskers off your chin?

To aid in our studies, we bought a microscope from a mortician's school, and with it we were able to examine our edges with magnification up to 500 power. And what did the edges look like? Well, *if the edge was really sharp,* we could see *no teeth whatsoever.* The only time we ever found a tooth, it was a defect in the edge, probably due to improper abrasives, defective steel, or a just plain lousy job of sharpening.

Once we were fortunate enough to study our edges and take some pictures with a 10,000-power electron microscope. The results were the same. The sharper the edge, the straighter it was, even under 10,000-power magnification.

As we stated before, there is no other field that is more ridden with old wives' tales and gimmickry than the sharpening field. Probably because everybody just writes about it, and no one studies it! In one of our next books we will go a little further into the study of the edge using the microscope. This will certainly help us to understand the edge more clearly and just what it is.

WHAT KIND OF HONES SHOULD I BUY?

First of all, we want to look at what a hone is, what it does, and why. A hone consists of many small, sharp protrusions that cut into the metal that is being ground on it. It will remove metal quickly or slowly, depending on variables such as hardness of the hone, grit of the hone, the speed at which the metal travels across the hone, etc. If you want a hone that removes more metal faster, get one with a coarse yet soft grit. You want a softer hone because as those little sharp protrusions become dull, they will break away from the hone and expose another sharp protrusion, allowing you to grind faster.

The fine hone is just the opposite. You want it as hard as possible, and the grit as fine as possible. This is because as the hard hone is used, it actually becomes finer than its grit indicates, because the sharp little protrusions do not break off, but become dull, and give a finer edge. For this reason, a used fine hone is better than a new one. Also, a new hone usually has a rough surface on it from the manufacturing process, so until this is smoothed off either by rubbing with another hone or by use, it will not reach its peak efficiency. As you look under a light at an edge made by a fine hone, it appears as a polished surface. However, if you take a look at this same edge under a microscope, you will see that there are microscopic scratch marks, which we call furrows.

When we first started experimenting, there was nothing more confusing than the subject of hones. We had relied upon the opinions of those who were reputed to know the subject, but many questions surfaced. It was a "known fact" that you couldn't possibly sharpen a knife with anything other than an Arkansas hone. But evidence seemed to be pointing in other directions. We looked for anything that claimed to be a hone, from all over the world, and with this collection we started our study.

We went into the tanning industry and the meat packing industry to do our testing, much of which was done by shaving our faces with identical knives. This method proved to be the best, because we could control it better, and that tender, sensitive face would never tell you a lie. Then these tests brought up other questions: Is a hone the only thing that will sharpen? Does it do the best job? How about diamond abrasives? How about a file? And coated abrasives? And what about manufactured hones?

Well, the diamond has a very good reputation. We know diamonds are very hard, and very expensive, too. It sounds as if they would have to be good. Diamond sharpening hones are actually a type of coated abrasive; they are a thin layer of diamond on a base steel. For sharpening, we found them to be a little too coarse for the fine edge, and very slow for the coarse grinding. They were certainly more durable than other coated abrasives, but they imparted no magic to the edge, as was claimed. We conclude that their best use is as a girl's best friend.

The file worked all right, but only for metal removal. It is like the diamond in that only the surface will do the cutting, and when it is worn and dull, you are finished. One of the applications where a file is almost exclusively used for sharpening is the chain saw. However, this is a little different, because it's used to sharpen a moving edge, which cuts a solid, stable material, and we'll need a lot more experimenting under our belts before drawing any conclusions on it. However, there is little doubt that there could be a better edge put on a chain saw, especially for competition or the logger who wants the ultimate chain saw.

Coated abrasives proved to be interesting. They are a thin layer of abrasive on a base, which could be paper, cloth, or just about anything. Again, as with the diamond and the file, it is just the surface that does the cutting, so it is the surface that is important. However, it is interesting to note that the fine coated abrasive seems to get better as it is used, as the fine hone did. The fine coated abrasive also seemed to give a slightly better edge than the fine hone did.

We learned something interesting about manufactured hones, and that is you can have them made to your own specifications. Just write down what you want, and right or wrong, an abrasive company will make it up for you. But here comes the problem. What do you order?

Grit sizes range from under 50 grit to over 1,000 in some cases. Then there are the hardness code letters to consider, which range through the alphabet. You also have different types of bonds. There was no information available, because manufacturers had no reason to try making a fine hone. So we just picked numbers and letters at random and told the abrasive company to make some hones. Boy, what a mess! We got a bunch of laughs out of it, and a little poorer, but gradually we caught on to the idea and the results were very good.

We were always trying to get finer and finer with our hones. Once while talking over an order with the engineering department of one abrasive company, we found there was an abrasive we hadn't yet tried. It was optical flour, the material used in the making of lenses. "Make us a dozen hones from optical flour." "Can't do that, sorry." "How come?" "Too fine. Have problems with the hones splitting in the kilns." "Make them anyhow." "Can't be done." "Don't say can't, just do it." "We'll try."

Not unexpectedly, the first set of optical flour hones were cracked, and the engineer called to say they were a total loss. We tried again, worked some bugs out, and finally got some hones that were good.

We found there is no magic in any hone—it's all just the abrasive. It doesn't matter if it's natural, man-made, diamond, ceramic, or just a file. What really counts is proper grit size, bond hardness, and application.

WHAT DOES OIL DO FOR SHARPENING?

Now this might come as a shock to you, and some of you may even want to make sure you're sitting down for this one, but if you use oil in sharpening, it will: Number one—cost you money. Number two—make a mess. Number three—give you an inferior edge. Yep, we know, everything you have ever read told you to have a 55-gallon drum of oil on hand to pour on your hone whenever you wanted to sharpen a blade, or you'd never get it sharp. Now don't feel bad, because we thought the same thing when we first started experimenting. Never will forget that case of whale oil some sharp salesman sold us, claiming it would do some special hocus-pocus on an edge.

We would really like to tell you a big, spectacular story about how we discovered as a result of brilliant experimenting that oil is just one more of the many old wives' tales about sharpening, but we don't tell fibs. (Well, not too many.) The fact of the matter is we just happened to stumble over this, as is true with so many of the things we have learned about sharpening. Seems like so many times we would try to study a certain subject, and the end result would be a big flop. But in the process we would many times stumble onto something we weren't really looking for, or maybe learn something we would store in the back of our minds for use further on down the road.

We encountered a problem with using oil when we first started demonstrating at sports shows around the country. How do you sharpen all those knives with all that oil? Heck, we could drown in oil! So rather than use oil, we just kept our hones clean as best we could, and thought we could always switch to a new hone when the dirty one quit working. But guess what. The hones just kept going . . . and kept going . . . and kept going. Both the coarse and the fine. And then we noticed something else. Our edges seemed to be better than when we were using oil. Strange, huh? So then we ran a series of tests and found it to be true: you get much better edges without the use of oil.

One day we got a call from a professional knife manufacturer asking us what we thought we could do for his edges in one of the largest beef packing plants in the world. We assured him we could do well, so the company picked us up and flew us out to their plant. When we got to the sharpening room, we found ourselves a corner to work in and started sharpening knives. The people out on the cutting lines thought the edges were great. The second day we were there, the superintendent came into the sharpening room to watch us, and, not surprisingly, asked, "How come you're not using oil?" We explained that we found the edges to be better without the use of oil. "But everybody uses oil to sharpen. Why don't you just try it and see what happens?" So we did. He brought in a can of oil, and we added a generous portion to our hones. It wasn't that long afterward when he came back into the sharpening room. "Something is going wrong. The guys out there are complaining about that last batch of knives. What do you think happened?" We questioned him a little about the complaints and then told him we thought the problem was the oil. So we went back to clean hones and started sharpening again. A short while later, the superintendent came back and reported that his butchers were once again happy with their knives.

The question is, why did the edges deteriorate so quickly when we used oil? The answer is this. The grit that has been worn from the hone becomes suspended in the oil with the metal filings from the blade, and you get a grinding compound, similar to the stuff used to grind the valves on your car. Running your knife through this compound is like running it through a pile of sand. The edge comes into direct contact with the abrasive, and you get a poor edge. (Any edge coming in direct contact with a hard object, such as an abrasive, is in trouble.)

A typical example of this would be a farmer's plow. When it is new, it is reasonably sharp, but from there it just goes downhill. The reason the plow gets dull is that the abrasive passes over *both* sides of the blade—if there was contact on only one side, it would sharpen itself.

So we have now learned that when abrasive material passes *over* the top of the edge, you are "plowing," and consequently ruining your edge. Oil greatly contributes to this plowing effect, as do hones that are not clean. And because edges are microscopic, this is especially true of the fine hone. Now this would not apply if you had a constant flow of clean oil that would continuously wash the particles away. But what a mess you would have. The same theory applies to water, only you won't have quite the mess because the water will eventually evaporate.

After our experience in that packing plant with the oil we went into further study on the subject. We used electron microscopes with magnifications of up to 10,000 power, and you could easily see the difference between the wet and dry edges. The edges that had been sharpened in oil had small chips knocked out of the cutting edge; the dry-sharpened blades did not.

None of the machines we supply to the packing industry uses oil, and these machines sharpen the knives of thousands of professionals every day. So the next time someone tries to sell you oil for your sharpening, just tell him to stick it in his crankcase—like we should have told the whale oil salesman.

AT WHAT ANGLE SHOULD I SHARPEN?

There has been much confusion concerning sharpening angles. Much of this is due to writers who want to sound as if they have found all the answers. Like if you sharpen a this, you have to use a 22-degree angle, or if you sharpen a that, you must sharpen at a 19-degree angle. Can't you just see someone trying to keep a 19-degree angle, or for that matter any other exact angle, by hand? Now that would really be a steady hand.

Actually, the rule of thumb is to keep your blade under a 25-degree angle to your hone. Generally, the less the angle, the better your edge will be. If you have a protractor, use it to see what this angle looks like. If you don't, just take a piece of paper with square edges—which are 90°—and fold it in half at the corner. You now have 45°. Fold the 45-degree angle in half and you have 22.5°. Now don't get all shook up by that exact-sounding figure, because we are just looking for something under 25° and we want you to know what it looks like. Remember, we want this to be our final, or primary, edge, as shown in Figure 1-2.

It is important that we thoroughly understand an edge face. The edge face is the flat surface that has been made by grinding on the abrasive. If your grinding was done by using some type of guide for control, it will appear flat and uniform, as shown in Figure 1-2. If the grinding was done free-handed, the edge face will appear to be more rounded, and will be a little more difficult to distinguish. However, the results are basically the same. Remember that this is a magnified view of a cross section of an edge, so what's pictured here is an edge the width of which, including both primary and secondary edge faces, could be 1/16 of an inch, or even less.

The primary edge face angle (Figure 1-2) is CAB, made up of edge faces AC and AB. This edge face could be so small as to require a good light to look at it, depending on how you designed your secondary edge faces. The two edge faces, AC and AB, form edge face angle CAB, and this is the actual cutting edge, which was made on the fine abrasive.

The secondary edge face, CD and BE, was made on the coarse hone. This is actually our *relief* for the primary edge face, and if you look at it under magnification you will notice the coarse "furrows" left by the grit of the coarse abrasive. When two edge faces are used in sharpening, you have what is called "double-edging," which is a foolproof method of sharpening. Now let's go a little further and study this all-important double-edging to see how it works. Let's go to Figure 1-3.

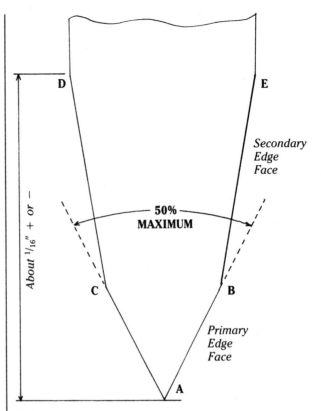

Figure 1-2

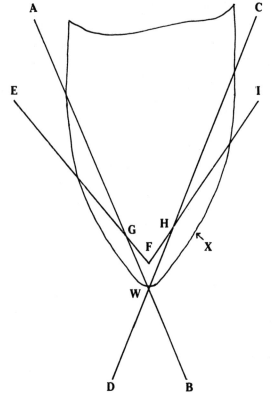

Figure 1-3

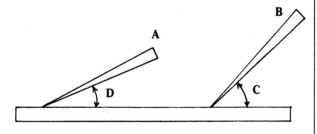

Figure 1-4

In Figure 1-3 the original, and very dull, rounded edge is indicated by line X. We are first going to grind in a secondary edge face CD with our coarse hone. Achieving this, we turn the blade over and grind in secondary edge face AB, thus giving us edge angle AWC. The edge will now have a *burr* (explained in more detail later) on it and will be very rough, which is certainly never satisfactory for any cutting purpose. So far, we have used only the coarse abrasive to remove excess metal, which leaves the edge face with very rough furrow marks. We now have our secondary edge, so our next step is to grind in the primary cutting edge. To do this, we go to our fine abrasive and increase the grinding angle just slightly. To get a better idea of what this double-edging looks like, let's go to Figure 1-4.

When we first started grinding the original edge shown in Figure 1-3, our grinding was done on the coarse abrasive at angle D shown in Figure 1-4. Now, to get our primary edge face, we must increase the angle very slightly—just a few degrees, but enough to give the secondary edge face clearance. Now we go to our fine hone, and why? Because the fine hone does not have the ability to remove much metal.

If we were to continue on the fine hone at the same angle we used to get the secondary edge face, we could grow old before we got a good edge. However, when we increase the angle on the fine hone, giving the secondary edge face proper clearance, the primary edge will set very quickly. As you can see in Figure 1-4, we used angle D on the coarse abrasive, then increased to angle C on the fine hone. This gives us cutting angle GFH (Figure 1-3), and if it's less than 25°, we will have a super edge.

WHY DO BUTCHERS USE STEELS?

If we ever got into a confusing subject in the field of edges, it's the subject of steels and steeling. When we first became familiar with the steel and its numerous problems, we thought we had hit on a question that had no answer. No matter who we asked, we couldn't get a satisfactory answer, and we soon realized that not only did we not know why a butcher uses a steel, the butcher didn't either. A typical steel is a rod, usually having an abrasive surface, that a butcher keeps at his side to sharpen or touch up his knife edge. He slides his knife down the surface of the steel, alternating sides, and is said to be "steeling" his edge. And there are just all kinds of steels. Thick ones, thin ones, round ones, flat ones, square ones, tall ones, short ones. And some people claim that you have to rub them smooth, while others tell you to soak them in vinegar. One guy said to run it between two roller skate wheels. Some said steel lightly, some said hard. Some use considerable angle, while others steel flat.

Well, all of this pointed to one thing—confusion! So this is when we started a long program into the study of the steel and its effects. We would watch men steeling while they were working, and tried to tell what the difference was between the professional who always had a good edge and the one who didn't. This led to more confusion, because at first there seemed to be no difference between the two, but much time and study proved that there was a difference. Careful study showed, for instance, that most men steel with a very shallow angle on the top of their steel, but a very steep one on the bottom, which will result in a poor edge. Also, the better butchers with the better edges used a smooth steel, while the others used just about everything.

Actually, if you don't have a good edge on your knife to begin with, steeling is going to do you very little good, if any, no matter what kind of steel you're using or how you're using it. So first you have to produce a good edge with the proper hones, that is, a very coarse hone to remove metal followed by a very fine hone to set the edge. Since you set your edge on a very fine hone, it only makes sense to use a very smooth steel. If you use a coarse steel you will just erase what you have done on the fine hone, because you must use progressively finer abrasive to get the ultimate edge. When you use a coarse steel after coming off a very fine abrasive, you're taking several steps backward.

The purpose of steeling your edge is twofold. First of all, it puts a very fine finishing touch on the edge, and secondly, it maintains the sharpness of the edge while in use. Keeping an edge sharp requires frequent steeling. If you do not steel properly you will lose the edge, and then the smooth steel will not bring it back, so you must start all over with your coarse and fine abrasives.

If you are considering buying a steel and want to do it right, consider only the smooth. The rule of thumb is to start with a good edge, and then *steel very lightly* on a *smooth steel.* Never steel rapidly, but use slow, carefully studied strokes. This subject will be covered in further detail in Chapter 2.

Teaching butchers to steel properly and ironing out steeling problems is by far the most demanding job when setting up a central sharpening system. We have found that somewhere between 2 percent and 5 percent of the people in the packing industry can be considered outstanding with a steel. A small handful are just so-so when it comes to steeling, and the rest of them just struggle through their eight hours a day, fighting their knife. You will find that it is well worth your time to study and learn the proper way to steel your edge.

HOW CAN I TELL IF AN EDGE IS SHARP?

Strange how we have something to measure everything. We have a tape to measure an exact eight-foot two-by-four when we are cutting studs. We have a quart container to measure exactly how much oil we are putting into our crankcase. And if we are grinding down a piece of metal, we can use a micrometer to measure thousandths of an inch. But now we have something different in our hands. We have been working on our knife for what seems like an hour, and now we want to see if it is sharp. Obviously, we have a problem.

The measuring tape is surely not going to help us. Neither is the micrometer, and you can obviously forget about the quart container. This is a whole new ballgame.

There are a number of ways to tell if an edge is sharp, but unfortunately most of them require considerable experience. This was another of the problems facing us when we first started experimenting with edges. How could we tell what we were doing if we couldn't somehow test or measure the edges?

We were very fortunate because the Missus had the uncanny ability to tell if a knife was sharp or not. She very simply "thumbed" the edge by letting the knife edge cut into her fingerprints to a point where you could see the cut, but where it would hardly reach the base of the print. In this way she could accurately grade an edge. Whenever we ran tests we would run to her with the knives to see how we had done. You could even tell by her expression how sharp the edge was. If she shivered a little when she touched the edge, we knew it was a home run

without her even saying a word. But if the side of her nose and mouth went up a little, it was back to the drawing board—or rather, abrasive. Where she got this talent we'll never know, but it was most valuable as our first accurate method of testing and grading an edge.

We used another method that seemed to work well, and that was shaving hair from the arm. You can tell quite a lot about what an edge is like by the way the hairs pop off when the edge contacts them. This method is used quite frequently in the packing industry by the older and better professionals. If you are going to test your edge by shaving, however, we must caution you to use extreme care. Also, shaving works better if you go down the arm, or with the "grain" of the hair. Shaving with a knife is something we do not recommend, but we go into it further in Chapter 2 for those of you who are going to do it anyway.

From shaving the arm, we got more adventuresome and started shaving something much more difficult and tender—our face. The face is quite a tender spot, and the whiskers are like tough little wires. If we were testing a hone, we would sharpen identical knives on various hones, lather up, and begin shaving a little at a time, first with one knife and then the other. The knives were marked, but we were unaware of which one was being used, so that a certain hone or method would not be favored. Because of the tenderness, this method of testing was more accurate than shaving the arm or leg.

Sometimes you will see other methods of testing an edge. Perhaps you have seen a barber run the edge across his fingernail to test its value. This is the method we first used, and it seemed to tell something about the edge, but far from the whole story.

Once in a while you will see some pretty weird things being done to test edges, and we'll never forget the experience we had at one of the sports shows. We were busy sharpening knives that people had brought in to us; one particular knife was a large hunting knife, its owner being very interested in knives and sharpening. We sharpened the knife and shaved a few hairs from the arm. He was very impressed, but said, "I use a different way of testing a knife." Then he stuck out his tongue and was just about to run the knife across it when we hollered, so loud in fact that it startled the guy, and he just stood there with his knife held up, and his tongue hanging out. Much to our relief, the tongue slipped back into his mouth, and the knife went back into the sheath. Just no telling what would have happened if he had run that knife over his tongue. If nothing else, he would have found out what a sharp knife will do to a tongue!

Perhaps the best way to test an edge is by using an Edge Tester, as shown in Pictures 1-2 and 1-3. This is a special tool that our company has developed and it provides a foolproof way for anyone to test an edge, from the housewife to the professional butcher. They are widely used in the packing industry by the people working in the sharpening rooms, as well as by management to keep tabs on the performance of the sharpening room. If there is ever a complaint out on the cutting line about the sharpness of the edges, it is quite simple for management to check for themselves whether the complaint is valid or someone is just trying to give the sharpening people a hard time.

Another method of testing an edge is to use the knife for its intended purpose. If you are going to be cutting meat, then it's best to test the knife in meat. We have seen numerous cases where a knife will cut differently in different materials. For instance, an edge that feels super in cutting leather may not feel so great when you're cutting meat. So the ultimate test, then, is whether

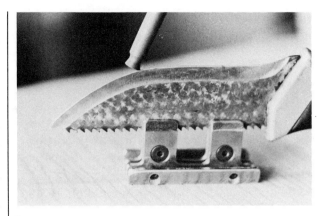

Picture 1-2 *The first step in testing an edge is to determine whether there are any nicks or burrs. To do this, hold the Edge Tester™ at one end, and then push it over the edge. A properly sharpened edge should feel silky smooth over its entire length.*

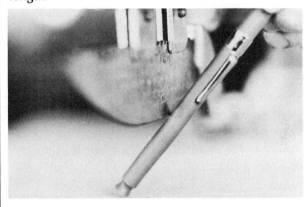

Picture 1-3 *Now we have to determine whether the edge is really sharp. To do this, set the Tester on a flat surface and then hold it at a 45-degree angle to that surface. Now hold your blade in a vertical position and lightly rest it on the surface of the Tester. If the edge is sharp, it will "bite" into the Tester with just the weight of the knife; if the edge is dull, it will slide down the surface of the Tester. The Edge Tester™ is available only from Razor Edge Systems, Inc., P.O. Box 150, Ely, MN 55731.*

the edge will cut properly in the material it is to be used on.

WHAT ABOUT SERRATED EDGES?

We are seeing more and more serrated edges, and the question comes up of how good they are, if indeed they are any good at all. Serrated edges do have a place, and in their place they do a good job. Their place is sometimes in the kitchen, but mainly in the restaurant. You all associate a serrated knife with a steak. Whenever you go into a restaurant and order a steak, you can always tell how tough the steak is going to be by the knife they give you. If you get an ordinary knife, you're in luck, because your steak is going to be tender. However, if you are so unfortunate as to get a serrated knife with your steak, you know your jaw muscles are in for a good workout.

Well, there are other reasons for a serrated knife, too. Let's suppose that someone takes a knife and cuts a piece out of their steak. Chances are that they just cut 50 percent steak and 50 percent ceramic plate. An ordinary edge would just fold as it was run over the plate, and thereafter its cutting efficiency would be greatly diminished. Not so with the serrated blade. This is because just the tips of the serrations touch the plate, keeping the remainder of the serrations above the hard surface, thereby protecting them. No matter how the knife is abused, you will always have something that will rip its way through a steak. So you can see that in a kitchen or restaurant serrated knives can do a good job, but this is the only place we have ever seen them used effectively. We have never seen them used professionally, as they would just not be suitable. Actually, they don't cut the meat; they tear their way through it.

While demonstrating our sharpeners at one of the sports shows, we asked the crowd if anyone had a knife they wanted sharpened. There was a fellow standing in front of our booth wearing a very fancy set of holsters. He reached back behind his holster, slid out a knife, handed it to us, and asked, "What can you do with this?" It was a well-known serrated knife, and it was new. We took a piece of leather, handed it to him, and told him to cut it. "What do you think of the edge?" we asked. "Sharp." So then we sharpened it—just the tips of the serrations—handed it back to him with the leather, and asked him to cut it again. "Wow, really good." Then we handed him one of our sharpened knives. He took one cut at the leather and his eyes lit up like a lamp. We asked, "Now, do you want to keep your serrated edge, or would you rather have an edge like ours?" "Like yours, for sure!" So we ground off the serrations and sharpened it like our display knife. He tried the new edge on the leather and he was just delighted. "Thanks," he said. "That's great." He then reached back to slip the knife back into its pouch—and in the process he cut right through his nice, new, fancy holster!

ARE KNIVES SHARP WHEN YOU BUY THEM?

Nope, not really. And this doesn't apply just to knives, either. It applies to anything that has a cutting edge, be it a chain saw, plane, ax—you name it. When it comes from the factory it's as dull as all get out, and we usually refer to it as a "blunt instrument." Now this doesn't mean that the inexperienced wouldn't judge it to be sharp. We are talking about the professional who earns his living with his tools. We have never seen a professional meat cutter who would use a new blade before he sharpened it, unless he was very inexperienced.

Why, then, are tools made like this? After all, the heart and soul of the tool is its edge, so why make a nice chain saw, and then add a poor edge as sort of an insult to the tool? Well, we don't really know the reason for this, and can only speculate.

The main reason seems to be the same reason the builder of the hospital doesn't perform the operations. It's an entirely different profession. We have found that companies that manufacture tools with cutting edges are very reluctant to change their habits. Although they may claim to have the ultimate edge on their tools, they actually have little interest in perfecting their edges.

Knife manufacturers always advertise that they have the sharpest edges in the world, but when you pick up most any knife and check its edge, you wonder if perhaps the sharpener didn't show up that day. Old customs die hard in American industry, and it seems we have the attitude that if it worked yesterday, it's going to be good enough for tomorrow, too. We fight change and resist new ideas, and are more concerned with the bottom line of this month's balance sheet than we are with the future. But change we can, and change we must, so we can hope to find a better edge on products in the future.

WHAT DO YOU ADVISE ABOUT SAFE KNIFE HANDLING AND USAGE?

Knife safety is something that is many times overlooked, and it really shouldn't be. This is true not only with the young hunter, but also with the veteran knife handler. As with most dangerous things, if we develop safe habits in using them, we greatly decrease the chances of getting hurt.

There is an old idea in the packing industry that you can always tell a butcher by his hands—plenty of scars. But not really. The smart butcher gets one bad cut and he learns to respect the tool he is using. It seems that cuts come from inexperience and carelessness. Usually the older veterans don't suffer many cuts because they have learned their lesson, and are more cautious. And it's not just the hands that suffer the cuts. We were in a packing plant once when a worker stabbed himself in the upper part of the leg, partially severing the large artery that supplies blood to the leg. It was only the quick action of the men who rushed him to the hospital that saved his life.

If we were to pinpoint the main cause of cuts, it would have to be what we call "slips," so let's go into this a little.

Many people think that a sharp knife is a dangerous knife, and as it gets duller, it gets safer. False. It's the unloaded gun and the dull knife that will give you the business. Obviously, part of this is due to no respect. You respect the loaded gun, and you respect the sharp knife, so you are more careful. But there is another culprit hiding in the shadows here, just waiting for a mistake, and it's the slip.

Let's say you are boning out a carcass. If your knife is very sharp, you can cut effortlessly. The sharp knife is easy to guide, and also pulls effortlessly through the meat. Your arm and muscles are relaxed as you work, because you are not making a strenuous effort. Now let's suppose something happens, and your edge suddenly goes dull. It's a different story now. Instead of being effortless to guide, cutting becomes much more difficult, and you now must put considerable push behind your knife. Instead of being relaxed, your muscles are now wound up tight like a spring, and you have lost much of your control.

Just as an example, take a pencil and write your name. Feel the muscles in your arm and notice how relaxed they are. Now squeeze your pencil as you write your name again. Now, as your muscles have tightened up, you have also lost much control and accuracy in your writing. The more your muscles tighten up, the more accuracy and control you lose. And the same thing is true with a knife, only the end result is not just a scribbled name.

When your blade gets dull, it will hang up, or refuse to move with the pressure you are now using. So what do you do? You simply add more pressure. And this is on a hand and arm that is already tired from being overexerted and has lost much of its control. Suddenly the knife lets go, and with the extra power and speed behind it, it can become devastating, not only to the person using the knife, but to anyone who might be in the area helping or just observing.

Now if that knife had been sharp in the first place, the hand and arm would not be tired, accuracy and control would not suffer, and most important, the knife probably would not have hung up in the first place, but would have continued cutting effortlessly.

Whenever the opportunity presented itself, we tried to look into knife accidents in the packing industry and usually found the culprit to be a dull knife. Experienced men in the industry will always say that a dull knife is the reason for most serious cuts. Incidentally, the man who cut the artery in his leg was a victim of a knife that hung up and slipped. So keep it sharp, and keep it safe!

Another common reason for cuts is keeping the knife in the hand while doing something other than cutting. Say you are skinning out your deer and you want to pull on the hide for some reason. Instead of taking the time to lay the knife down and then pull the skin, you simply grab the skin with both hands, the knife still in one of them, and then give a big jerk. If the skin lets go unexpectedly, you are in big trouble. Or if

your cold, greasy hands slip off, same result. You end up with a nasty cut, probably out in the woods someplace where medical help is a long way away. Certainly a sad ending to a successful hunting trip. So never have your knife in your hands unless you are actually using it. If you have to push or pull something, put your knife down.

Another bad habit with a knife is doing something you shouldn't be doing with it. Like cutting the top off a can. This is a situation that encourages a slip, and a good many times the pressure is in the direction of yourself or another person. Use your can opener if you have one, but if you must use a knife for some reason, always apply the pressure *away* from you so that if it slips you'll just cut air, not you or your hunting partner.

When we were kids, we always had a jackknife in our pocket. It was usually the Boy Scout type, with all the little blades we never understood. But there was the main blade, and we all understood that, and used it frequently. One of the games we played was a game we called mumblety-peg. We did different things with our knife, and it was always supposed to end up sticking in the ground. But, of course, we just couldn't be satisfied with this, and it wasn't long before we were flipping the knife at the ground to see if it would stick. Then came other targets like oak trees, or the neighbor's garage, which was a favorite, or any other thing our villainous little minds could think of. And this brings us to our next subject, and a real big no-no with a knife.

Knife throwing, unless properly done with the proper equipment, is dangerous and also devastating on a knife. Mom just couldn't figure out where all of her knives were going, because we little brats would sneak them out of the kitchen and use them for throwing. Then it wasn't long before the blade snapped, or the handle fell off, so we had no choice but to destroy the evidence. So went mother's cutlery, and she never did find out. So let's keep our mumblety-peg to a minimum, and this especially applies to the long-distance variety.

Most knife safety is just good common sense, sort of the "think before you do it" kind. We obviously don't want to run with a knife in our hands, and we wouldn't climb a tree with our knife unsheathed. A good rule to follow is to keep your knife sheathed or folded if you are not using it.

And this brings up another subject, the folded knife. Ever wonder how many guys have ended up with a jackknife blade folded across their knuckles? Years ago we didn't have the safety feature of a locking blade, but now you see more and more of them around. Can't think of a more sensible safety feature in a folding knife, especially for the inexperienced person who is going to use his knife for just anything and everything. A little pressure in the wrong direction, and the blade can unexpectedly snap back over your knuckles. Ouch! This is one time when a dull blade would be the best blade by far. And the duller the better. Maybe as dull as a round piece of pipe.

Most cuts can be divided into two classes—real bad, and just the irritating kind. The bad ones usually come from slips, like a guy who cuts through a rope and into his leg. The irritating cuts are usually the kind we get when we stick our hands into the dish pan, forgetting we have a butcher knife in there. Neither cut is anything we want, and we can eliminate them almost entirely if we just keep our knives sharp and use a little common sense in handling them.

Also rather important, we should always "clear ourselves" when using a knife. For example, if the guy who cut through the rope and into his own leg had thought to clear his leg from the path of the knife in case he lost control, he would have cut a lot of air instead of his leg. This is true of any edged tool, whether it be knife, ax, or chain saw. Ask yourself: What happens if it goes all the way through unexpectedly? If the answer happens to be a part of your tender body, you had better make some changes.

There are times when you have to pull a knife toward you in a difficult place. In these cases you should pull with your shoulder, not your arm, especially if you are an inexperienced person with no protective equipment. The professional in a packing plant has to pull toward himself in many operations, but he is trained, and in case of a slip he wears a protective mesh apron to prevent injury. But if you're a hunter in the woods with no protective equipment, you must be cautious.

The more pressure needed to move the blade, the more important this becomes. Simply stiffen your hand and arm, and then pull with your shoulder and body until the dangerous cut has been completed. This way, if you do slip, the knife isn't going to go far because you are pulling with your shoulder. Contrast this to pulling with an arm that is wound up like a spring and you can imagine the difference.

Perhaps you have had experience with a knife accident, or maybe you know of some knife safety tips that we have not covered here. We would really appreciate hearing from you so we can pass them on in the future as we deal with people and continue writing books. Certainly everyone appreciates safety tips, and maybe yours will prevent someone from someday making a foolish mistake that could end up a disaster. Just write to us at the address at the back of the book, and all of us, as well as many other people, will give you a great big thank-you.

HOW DO YOU TELL A GIMMICK?

There is an old saying that goes, "If the darned thing won't sell, just tell the guy it's a knife sharpener." There is no field that is more swamped with gimmicks than the field of sharpening. Seems like everyone who wants to go into business thinks that making a sharpener is a good place to start. Drawers are full of gadgets that were bought because they promised to sharpen this or that. No sooner does one die off the market than it is replaced by two more. So the question is: How do we determine if a gadget or a kit will actually be a good investment? Simple. All we have to do is apply the knowledge we have learned, and we'll get our answer.

First of all, the ultimate test is how well it sharpens. If you can produce an edge that will be capable of shaving hair from the arm or leg, then the investment was worthwhile. You got what you paid for—a good sharpener. But what if you can't test it before you buy it, then what? Remember what is necessary to produce an edge: proper abrasive, proper angle, and proper technique.

If you're buying a sharpening kit, first of all check the hones. If one of the hones is very fine and seems to be rather heavy and dense, it's probably OK and would be suitable for setting the edge. The other hone should be very coarse and capable of rapidly cutting a blade. But what if it's in-between? Now you have a very questionable product, for it's an abrasive that is too fine to remove metal from a blade, and too coarse to set an edge.

Most hones just aren't what the vendor claims them to be, and many are sold as being able to remove metal, which they don't. We have never seen a natural stone that was suitable for removing excess metal from a knife. So how do you test whether this hone is going to be OK?

Just take your fingernail and run it across the surface; if it does a good job of biting into your fingernail, it will also do a good job of removing metal.

Many manufactured coarse hones tend to have a hard surface on them, making them seem finer than they really are. Once you wear through the hard surface it will seem coarser, and will cut better for you. A good way to check this is to find a grinding wheel that has been used enough to have the outer surface worn off. First run your fingernail over the unworn side of the wheel, and then over the worn grinding surface. The reason that the side of the wheel feels finer than the edge is because that hard coating has not been worn off.

On the other hand, if you are looking at a coated abrasive, similar to sandpaper, it will feel coarser when new, and as it is used will begin to feel finer, so you have to allow for this adjustment. Do a little experimenting with this, and you'll be much more familiar with abrasives.

If you're looking at one of those very small hones, don't buy it. Better save your money. Any hone that is less than 5 inches long and $1\frac{1}{2}$ inches wide is of little or no value. It is hard enough to get the proper stroke over a long hone, and shortening it will just compound your problem. And compound problems are just not the sort of thing you ought to be buying.

Now we come to the second necessity in sharpening, and that is proper angle. Proper angle, as well as angle control, is of the utmost importance. You can probably keep enough control by hand to obtain a usable edge. However, if you can use some type of control guide, the quality of your edge will jump like unreal. It doesn't matter if you are sharpening a scalpel or an ax, an angle control will do wonders for you. We will discuss this in more detail in Chapter 2.

We have a certain knife we have used for many years to shave the face, especially for testing purposes. Sometimes the knife gets left where it is a temptation to be picked up and used for things other than shaving, like skinning a rabbit or something. Well, if we're in a hurry to shave the next time, and just take the knife to the hone without a guide—wow! do we suffer. No matter how hard we try to sharpen by hand, that shave is just not going to be comfortable. That sharpening guide just makes a world of a difference.

Our third necessary sharpening ingredient is technique. If the sharpening device you're looking at seems to lack a good bit of information on sharpening technique, you can bet the reason is that the manufacturer just doesn't know how to do it, so he can't tell you.

There are some sharpening devices on the market that are of little or no value, especially for sharpening. Notably worthless is the one where you draw an edge between two hardened metal surfaces. As you draw your knife through, the steel disks peel off some of the edge, and what this does is make a very rough, weak burr on your edge. If you apply the rules you have learned, you can easily see that this gadget is a poor investment.

Another gimmick is the copy of the butcher's steel. We have never found a steel of this design to be of any value, unless it is extremely smooth. Many are just designed to be eye appealing, but it doesn't matter if they are large, pocket size, flat, round, short, or long; if they are anything but smooth, forget it. And a steel is not for obtaining an edge, but for *maintaining* an edge.

Sometimes you might see a dandy-looking little outfit that contains a fine abrasive for "touching up" the edge, what about that? Well, an edge that can successfully be touched up with a fine abrasive is a rare bird. When the edge is "lost" you always have to go back and start over with the coarse abrasive. Sometimes we see an edge touched up in the packing industry, but only by the best professionals, and even then the results are of dubious quality.

So remember, the three necessities for sharpening are proper abrasives, both very coarse and very fine; proper angle and control; and proper technique. Without all three of these, you may as well forget sharpening.

So now if you get stuck with a sharpening gimmick, you've got it coming, "Cuz ya know better, don'cha?" The barker always puts on an impressive demonstration as he shows his product, but the end result is usually the same—a frustrated sharpener. And one more gadget in the back of the drawer.

Well, that concludes the chapter on the questions most asked about sharpening, and we hope you have understood each answer. Do you feel like you are becoming more familiar with edges? By the time you finish this book you will be able to consider yourself an expert.

Many of you will likely have some questions of your own you would like answered, but please consider that we have neither the time nor the staff to handle your individual questions. However, if you feel there is an outstanding question or point we have not covered here, you can send it in to us for consideration in one of our future books, and then perhaps you will be benefiting many people.

THE THEORY OF SHARPENING

We are now ready to go into the theory of sharpening. Chapter 1 has already given you a substantial understanding of edges and how to use them, so this chapter should be fairly simple for you to understand. By all means, go through Chapter 1 again if you think it will help you. As we move through this chapter we will emphasize some of the most important points by relating some of our research experiences.

Before we can get into the actual sharpening, we first have to go into the basics of knife grinds. Many of these leave a lot to be desired, so we will expose some of these problems for you.

Blades begin as a sheet of steel, which is then punched out on a press to a basic blade design. We now have a blank with squared-off edges. Obviously, some kind of taper has to be ground on this blank to convert it from a strap of steel to a blade. But the question is, how should we grind it? Or if we have purchased a knife, what should the manufacturer have done with it?

Let's look at the knife blade in Figure 2-1. It has been cut in half so that we can look at a cross section, which is magnified in Figure 2-2. First we must determine what the blade is going to be used for and, even more important, how it is going to be used. If you are going to use the knife to open up 55-gallon drums, or abuse it in some other way, you are going to want a grind like angle 1A1. However, if you are going to use a knife as it is intended, you will want a grind that is closer to angle 3A3. And what do we call this grind? It's our old friend, relief, and you can rate it as the most important thing in sharpening. Again, relief is the thickness or thinness directly behind the cutting edge. It has significant effect not only on the ease of sharpening but on the quality of the edge.

CHAPTER 2

Fundamental and Advanced Sharpening Technique

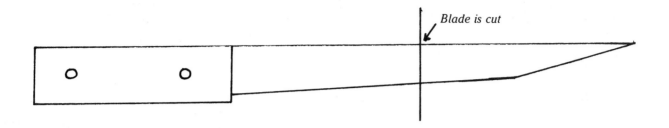

Blade is cut

Figure 2-1

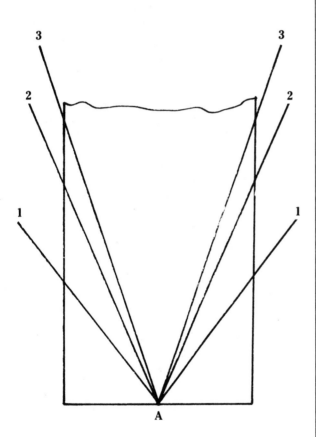

Figure 2-2

Regardless of the manufacturer, the relief on most knives can be rated from bad to awful. And don't let the manufacturer tell you that his knife is hard to sharpen because his steel is so terrific. Baloney. He simply just didn't do a good job of grinding his knife. Sure, you can chop your way into or out of anywhere without chipping the blade, but the problem is you'll sprain your arm just trying to clean out a deer, because it won't take a good edge.

Let's look at a few different types of knife grinds. It doesn't really matter what they look like, just as long as you get the desired results. Now remember, we are just considering the grind that should be on the blade *before* we even start sharpening.

In Figure 2-3, the grind in A would be OK if it would be continued down to the point indicated by the arrow. But that is the problem. The manufacturer usually grinds it off similar to angle V, and we have a very poor relief. In B, the blade grind would be great, but again it is usually cut off like angle V, and you are back to block one. C is the same as A, except that it is hollow ground. But it is too far back from the cutting edge to be effective, so hello again, block one. Why this grind is so widely used, we'll never know. And to make matters even worse, it is then usually rounded off at angle V. When these edges have been used awhile, and sharpened a few times, the problem gets worse—much worse.

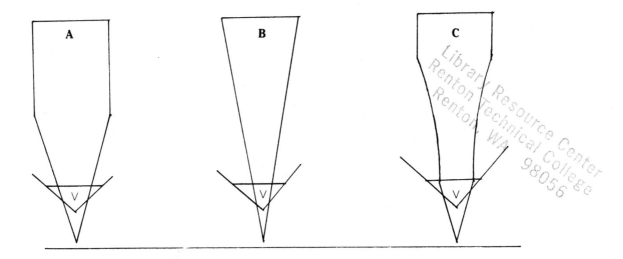

Figure 2-3

So what is the ideal relief in a knife blade? And how do we determine it? The rule of thumb for the professional is: as thin as possible, without experiencing damage to the blade. This is only for the professional or the person who wants the absolute ultimate in an edge. He will make the relief progressively thinner, until finally the blade starts to chip out as he uses it. Then he knows he has gone too far, and will slightly back off on his relief until he experiences no chipping. For the average professional this is a lot easier than it might sound.

We recommend a maximum thickness of .02 inches at the point one quarter of an inch behind the cutting edge, which isn't very much. Take a set of feeler gauges and see for yourself how thin .02 inches really is. As you can see in Figure 2-4, there is a considerable difference in actual relief in the hollow grind and in the straight grind, but most people do not have access to a hollow grinder. If you do a good job on your straight grind, though, you will be plenty happy with it. And if you want to get fancy, you can always put together a simple hollow grinder, which we will talk about a little later in this chapter.

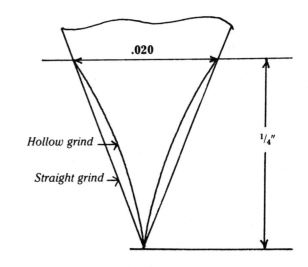

Figure 2-4

So we have just learned that the greatest fault of many a knife is its lack of relief. This is compounded by the fact that everyone always sharpens just on the cutting edge, with absolutely no thought given to improving the relief. The end result is that you have a hopelessly blunt instrument. But fear not! Instead, let's start from scratch. We'll correct not only the sharpener's mistakes, but the manufacturer's as well, and when we have finished we'll have a knife we are proud of and will be a joy to use.

First, we will scrub this blade in on a coarse abrasive to give us the desired relief. Don't be too concerned about any exact angle to begin with. Not everyone will agree to an exact angle, but everyone will certainly appreciate the slightest angle possible when they use the knife. In Figure 2-5, it would benefit us considerably if we ground our relief in as indicated by the dotted lines. To do this, place most of the blade pressure on the heel at point A, rather than on the cutting edge. Try grinding in a circular motion, using as much pressure as you wish. It's going to take you a while to correct everyone's mistakes, so be patient.

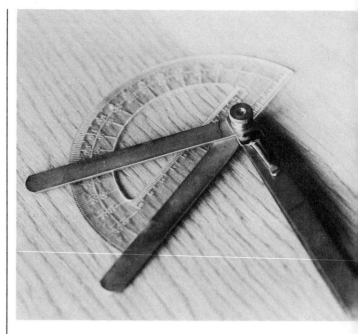

Picture 2-1

Before going any further, let's talk a little bit about angles. Use an angle duplicator and a protractor to check this, as shown in Picture 2-1. Just to give you some idea, the total edge angle on the ax we used to set the world championship was 20°, while a knife we have used to shave with at sports shows has a total edge angle of 12°. No attempt was made to get an exact angle on either the ax or the knife, but rather "just what looked OK." The reason we have a wider angle on the ax is because we also use it to chop with, and the edge must withstand shock. If it was tapered back too far, you would leave a chunk of your blade in some hardwood knot. Especially if it's frozen.

OK, back to our grinding. How do we know when to stop grinding in our relief? Well, for sure you ought to stop before grinding the blade down to the hilt. Now is a good time for you to

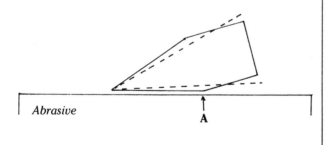

Abrasive   A

Figure 2-5

become friends with a burr. It will tell you one thing—STOP!

The burr is that rough, ragged, microscopic piece of metal that is turned up when *one side reaches the other*. The burr is always a foolproof way of determining when to stop, and that is why we always use it. Look at Figure 2-6, and you will get a better understanding of a burr. Learning to spot this burr is one of the most important steps in sharpening, if not the most important. Picture 2-2 shows the proper way to feel for a burr. Place your fingers lightly at about a 45-degree angle and draw your hand away from the cutting edge. Practice this, be patient, and study this until you understand it thoroughly, because it's *very important!*

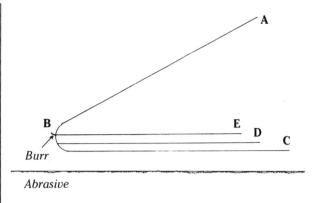

Figure 2-6

Here we have a microscopic drawing of an edge that has been worn, as is indicated by the rounded edge at point B. Angle ABC represents the original edge, which was then ground on the coarse abrasive until we got angle ABD. Notice that we have not met the other side as yet, so we must continue grinding until we reach what looks like angle ABE. We have now ground into the halfway point at the edge B, and we are beginning to form a burr. If you have a good magnifying glass you will be able to see the burr, but feeling for it is foolproof. Remember, the burr is always turned up from the hone. You must grind until you have a continuous burr running the entire length of the edge, and then flip your edge over and do the same on that side.

Remember, grinding in the burr is one of the most important *things in sharpening, so study this until you thoroughly understand it.*

Picture 2-2

There is another way to check the burr, and this is with your fingernail. One guy told us he couldn't use his fingernails. "How come?" we asked. "Cuz I bite 'em," he replied. Now that was a problem for this test. Anyhow, look at Figure 2-7 and try this method of feeling for a burr.

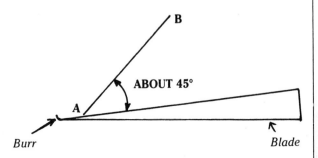

Figure 2-7

Line AB represents the fingernail. Place your fingernail back on the blade at about 45°, and move slowly toward the edge. If there is a burr at the edge, you should be able to feel it.

It is always a good idea to stop frequently when you are sharpening your blade to check your progress. At first, feeling for your burr will seem strange to you, but gradually you will catch on. When you feel your first burr, you'll probably hit the ceiling with joy, and you'll have a right to celebrate because you are well under way on your sharpening project.

If you have an 8X or 10X glass, this is a handy way to study your edge. You will notice how the abrasive is grinding away on certain spots on your blade, and how those rough grind marks we call furrows must extend all the way to the edge, as shown in Picture 2-3.

Picture 2-3

OK, after a lot of scrubbing on our abrasive we have finally detected a burr, and we now have an edge that looks like line ABE in Figure 2-6.

Now we want to make an important point. Pay attention because we are going to ask some questions later! *Always* taper your blade back a little each time you sharpen it, to keep it in top condition.

One of the advantages of a relief that has been hollow ground is that less metal will have to be removed when sharpening, as you can see back in Figure 2-3. There are all kinds of grinds, and it seems the manufacturer tries to make the blade have eye appeal, whether it makes for a good edge or not. But don't let them throw you. Just do your book learnin' here and you'll be able to turn the worst blade into something so good you won't believe it.

Now that we have properly prepared the relief of our knife, we can get into the actual sharpening. Now how do we go about sharpening? And what makes the difference between successful and unsuccessful sharpening? Or a good job and a poor job? And what were the three things we said were necessary to sharpen successfully every time? These are some of the things we will get into later when we do our actual sharpening.

THE SINGLE BEVEL BLADE

If ever there was confusion in the art of sharpening, it surrounds our next subject—the single bevel blade. In trying to sharpen one of these blades and make it work, it seems everyone just throws their hands up in despair; then they throw the blade into the trash can; and finally, they go out and buy a new one. But strangely, the new one just isn't that great either when you compare it to what it should be. The truth is, the single bevel blade isn't that bad if you can get the idea of it straight.

Some examples of single bevel blades are scissors, saws, wood chisels, plane blades, and jointer blades. We live in an area where there are many ice augers, and everyone just throws the dull blades away rather than sharpening them. Let's find out what the big bogeyman is in this blade.

In Figure 2-8 we have the typical single bevel blade. The cutting edge at point C is formed by faces BC and CD. Most blades, and particularly the single bevel blades, come from the manufacturer with a poor relief, and should be tapered back to look more like angle ECD.

The secret key to the success of sharpening a single bevel blade is that you *never* touch a hone to side CD, unless the hone is perfectly flat

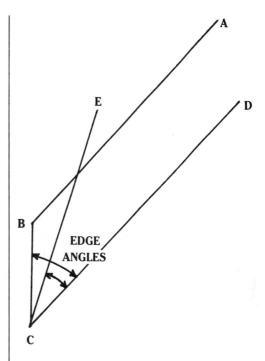

NEVER touch an abrasive to side CD unless it is parallel to the side, and then ONLY a fine abrasive.

Figure 2-8

or parallel to CD. This is the big sin, and it's why nobody can sharpen this very simple edge.

In Figure 2-9 we can vividly see the problem. Someone has put an abrasive to side CD. Notice how the cutting edge is sitting up in the breeze, while the rounded section of CD is where actual contact is. So many are frustrated because their single bevel blade seems sharp, yet won't cut. It could even shave easily, but if the cutting edge isn't the contact point on the material to be cut, you are going nowhere.

Another factor that could give you about the same results is wear, which will also remove metal and give you the same rounded effect. This is especially true in machine-driven single bevel blades. But this is not a serious problem because all you have to do is grind that radius away so that you end up with angle EFD, and then you're all set.

In the single bevel *nonmoving* blade, such as the wood chisel, we use a sharp blade and rely upon the material to cooperate with us and stand still while we cut it, such as chiseling a hole in a plank, or planing down a board. But what would happen if the material we were trying to cut wasn't rigid enough? For instance, a piece of cloth, or feathers for a fishing jig, or a field of wheat. Imagine what it would be like to go to the barber and have him cut your hair with his straight razor. This is where you have to put two blades together, giving you the single bevel *moving* blade, such as the scissors. One blade holds the material you're cutting in place, while the other whacks it off.

Single bevel moving blades are very common, and can be operated by hand, like a scissors or tinsnip, or they can be machine-operated, like a farmer's mower. Putting two blades against each other will pose a few more problems, but they require no special hocus-pocus if you just understand a few things.

Now don't get the idea that one blade is always dull, while the other is always sharp. Al-

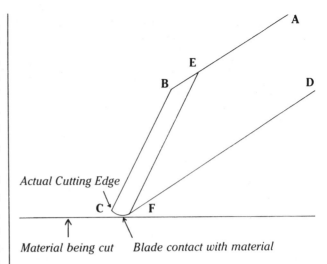

Actual Cutting Edge

Material being cut   *Blade contact with material*

Figure 2-9

though this is sometimes the case, generally it is better by far to have both blades sharp. However, if you aren't careful, you will have the problem of one blade "eating" the other, and then you end up with two dull blades. Self-destruction, I guess you'd call it. Figure 2-10 will give you an idea of how this happens. We can see how in the sharpening process a slight edge was left turned toward the other blade. On contact these two edges will destroy each other. Then we would not actually be cutting our material

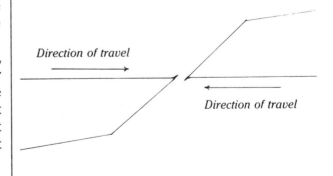

Direction of travel

Direction of travel

Figure 2-10

as we should be, but would be pinching it off, as shown in Figure 2-11. Very inefficient. To prevent this, we must make certain that the edges are not tilted toward each other, but rather just slightly away from each other.

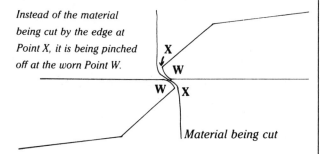

Instead of the material being cut by the edge at Point X, it is being pinched off at the worn Point W.

Material being cut

Figure 2-11

Notice in Figure 2-12 how both edges contact each other properly at the material line for a perfect cut. Now look at Figure 2-13, where we have either an improperly sharpened blade, or a severely worn edge. Notice how the cutting edge has changed from point W, where it should be, to points X and Y. And we can see that the blades do not contact each other at the cutting edge, but behind it, at points V and Z. Now, instead of cutting, which is smooth and accurate, we are actually crushing the fibers of ma-

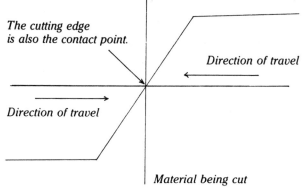

The cutting edge is also the contact point.

Direction of travel

Direction of travel

Material being cut

Figure 2-12

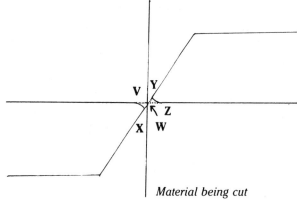

Material being cut

Figure 2-13

terial we are cutting, resulting in a rough, ragged edge.

We hope this has given you a good understanding of the single bevel blade. We will cover this blade further when we get into the sharpening section of this book, and then you will be an expert, and will no longer have problems with this very simple blade.

STEELING YOUR EDGE

One thing that seems to puzzle an awful lot of people is the proper way to steel your edge. You would be surprised at how many professional butchers don't even know how to do it! The reasons for steeling are twofold. First of all, it puts that finishing touch on the edge, and secondly, it maintains the sharpness of the edge as you use it.

As we mentioned earlier, for the best results you must have a very good edge to start with, and then your steel must be very smooth. In order to keep your edge sharp, you must remember to steel at frequent intervals. If you use your edge for too long a period of time, and it starts to feel dull, it is probably too far gone for the steel to do any good. However, if you steel regularly, your edge will stay sharp over a long period of time. For instance, we were in a packing plant where a butcher was boning hams, and we had him steel his edge upon completion of each piece. We had seen some operations where a knife would only last about fifteen minutes and it was too dull to cut butter. But when we worked with that man and taught him our steeling methods, the life of that edge jumped from fifteen minutes to over four hours.

The thing to remember in steeling is to be *very light,* and to *maintain a constant angle* throughout the steeling stroke. In Figure 2-14 you can see what we mean. The angle you start with at the hilt of the blade should be the same angle you end up with at the end of your stroke, when you are out on the tip of the blade. You must use the same angle again when you steel the other side of the edge.

Picture 2-4 *Use your fingers and wrist to get the proper steeling angle, and then "lock" your hand into this position. With your hand locked into position, use your elbow as the pivot point and drop the whole arm.*

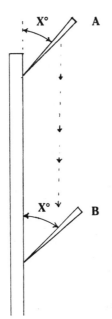

Steeling angle at beginning of stroke, in A, should be the same at the end of stroke, in B.

Figure 2-14

Your steeling will be much easier if you have an angle guide at the tip of your steel, as shown in Picture 2-4. Now all you have to do is lay your blade flat against this guide, and then maintain this angle throughout the stroke.

Rather than holding the steel in your hand, you may find it a big help if you mount the steel in front of you. This will allow you more freedom and will enable you to watch what you are doing so that you can be sure you are steeling properly.

One method is to use a steel mounted in a base, as shown in Pictures 2-5 and 2-6. This will be ideal if you are doing your cutting on a bench top or tabletop. Just place the steel where it will

Picture 2-5 *With the steel mounted in front of you, it's very easy to use and much more accurate than when holding it in your hand. In Picture 2-5 Mary just reaches out and places the blade against the angle guide, which gives her the exact steeling angle. Note the light touch she uses in handling the knife.*

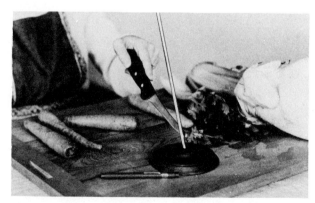

Picture 2-6 *Here Mary is way out on the tip of the blade but still has the same angle she started with. This is because she locked her hand into position and used her elbow as a hinge to get downward motion. Very simple, but very effective.*

be out of your way for working, but can still be easily reached for effortless steeling.

If you hang your game on a tripod to cut it up, try to mount your steel somewhere at about shoulder height. Make a hole at about 45° to the ground and push your steel into it. Don't worry about its being real sturdy, because you won't be using much pressure against it anyway. Before you mount the steel, study your work area. You don't want the steel to be in the way when you are working, but you still want it close enough so all you have to do is reach out for it. You will also want the angle guide at the tip of the steel to be clearly visible.

Now all you have to do is reach out and put your knife against the angle guide, and then "lock" your fingers and wrist in this position (Picture 2-5). Use your shoulder as the pivot point, and *slowly* drop your forearm so that the entire edge makes contact with the steel (Pictures 2-5 and 2-6). When you reach the end of the stroke and are out on the tip of your blade, take note of the angle you have. Is it the same angle you had at the top of your steel? If you didn't move your fingers or wrist, but only your shoulder, you should still have the same angle. Practice this stroke until you have it mastered, concentrating on using a *very light* touch, and maintaining a *constant angle* throughout the stroke. Alternate from one side to the other, using the same angle on both sides. After two or three strokes on each side of the edge you are ready to go back to work. As you become experienced at this, steeling your edge will seem like second nature, but until then always use very slow, carefully studied strokes. If you have a good edge to start with, you will find the results of this steeling method to be just fantastic.

We set up a sharpening system once in a packing plant that had four boning lines, each with a capacity of about eighty head per hour. We mounted steels in front of the meat cutters in much this same fashion, and the results were spectacular. Men and women who previously struggled through eight hours a day with a dull knife suddenly had knives that were as sharp, if not sharper, than the top butchers in the plant. This was a blow to the egos of those top butchers, because they were no longer "top knife." Mounting the steels out in front was the great equalizer. Sore arms, wrists, and hands were cured, as these people could now keep a sharp knife all day long, and a sharp knife pulls much easier than a dull one.

So carefully study your steeling, and you will be elated with the results.

BUILD YOUR OWN HOLLOW GRINDER

One of the handiest little machines we ever had was the one we made for hollow grinding. We used it for many years and it worked super. One of the best things about it was that it was very inexpensive to make, which was vital when we started and when everything we used for our experimenting was something that we either had made or found in a junkyard. And it probably worked just as well as something we could have purchased. Just goes to show that you don't have to have a fortune sunk into equipment to set up your own lab. Just a little imagination.

A hollow grinder is a machine that will give you a concave relief on your blade, as in this diagram:

Take a look at Figure 2-15. The motor we used is just a simple ¼ HP, like you might find in an old washing machine or dryer your neighbor threw out. The extension that goes on the shaft can be found at most any hardware store for only a few bucks. Use a coarse grinding wheel

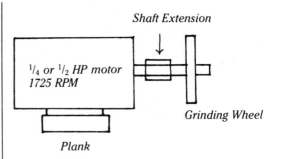

Figure 2-15

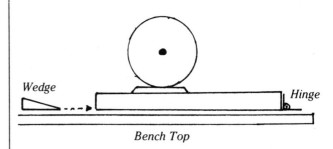

Figure 2-16

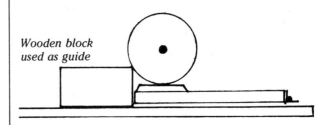

Figure 2-17

if you have it, but almost anything you have will do to get started.

If you'll notice, we use a motor with a low 1,725 RPM. Two good reasons for this. First of all, a lot of speed just heats things up. Secondly, a lot of speed just throws particles faster and farther, so keep the RPM down. If you can get below 1,725 RPM, do it. On some motors, you can just change wires around and get to about 800 RPM. If you are going to go from a motor to an arbor, gear it down. And use a good size plank under your motor to make it solid and stable.

In Figure 2-16 you can see how we have hinged our motor base so we can use a wedge to adjust the motor up and down. This way you can get just about any desired grinding angle, simply by raising or lowering the motor and grinding wheel. In Figure 2-17 we also have a wood block clamped in place to use as a guide.

And always remember something *very* important: *use eye protection!* If you are going to enjoy your newfound interest in sharpening, you need two good eyes. And something thrown up into your eyes from the grinding wheel can be a disaster, physically, mentally, and financially. We always use glasses *and* a large shield that covers the whole face.

Looking at Figure 2-18 now, notice how blade number 1 has almost a blunt grind on it. Blade number 2 has more angle to it; the farther down you go on the wheel, the better relief you get, as in blade number 3.

Now a word of caution. *Don't* ever use the under, or *down* side of the wheel (Figure 2-18). If you do, it will tend to draw your work into the wheel, and you could get hurt. Always use the up side of the wheel, which will tend to push the blade away, rather than drawing it into the wheel. In Figure 2-19 the ax is OK, because it cannot be drawn into the wheel.

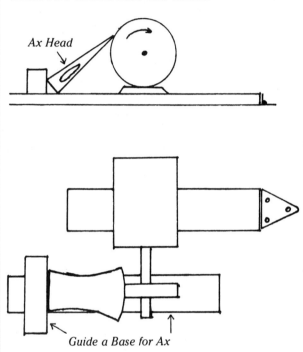

Ax Head

Guide a Base for Ax

Figure 2-19

In sharpening some tools you'll have to move your guide to the right or left so that you have access to the wheel with all of your blade. When you flip your blade over to grind the other side, you might have to come in on an angle in order to miss the motor with your knife handle, as shown in Figure 2-20. Notice how the guide block C is moved to the left in Figure 2-20 so that you can grind all the way to the hilt of your knife

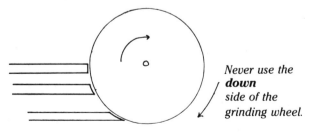

Never use the **down** *side of the grinding wheel.*

Figure 2-18

blade. Scissors would be the same. Just pull your edge straight across the wheel as in line B, the arrow indicating the handle. Then when you flip it to get the other side, you will probably have to come in on an angle as in line A. A pair of scissors, however, will require only a one-way stroke.

Whenever sharpening, always use a guide to enable you to keep a constant angle. This is a great deal of the battle. Also, when using your hollow grinder, do a little grinding on one side and then on the other, rather than grinding one side all the way down at once. Don't worry if your grinding doesn't look like much to begin with; it will look better and better as you go along.

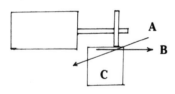

Figure 2-20   *As viewed from top*

This simple but very efficient machine will do a beautiful job on any single bevel or double bevel blade, and your first one should do you proud! You'll find many uses for your hollow grinder, and you'll get better with it as you use it. It'll become your third hand. It's terrific for your workshop, and if you are going to earn a few extra bucks sharpening tools, it will become essential. And you'll get a big bonus, too—it'll make you proud of your work.

Abrasive Wheel Safety

Let's touch briefly on the problem of a moving wheel kicking back the object we are placing against it. The softer the wheel, the more we have to worry about the problem. Rag wheels, as well as felt wheels, are notorious for this, especially when the wheel has an edge *or point* it can grab. Rag wheels can be made of felt or layers of cloth having a special surface that can grab the edge or point of a knife and throw it. And the sharper the edge or point the quicker it will grab it. This not only applies to a grinder, but to any situation where an edge is placed on a moving surface, as on a wood lathe.

If you can, make some type of guide that will prevent the wheel from grabbing the tool, especially with softer wheels. Figure 2-21 shows the side view of a simple but effective guard that helps prevent accidents. We've used this numerous times, but we're still careful, as it's the unexpected that's dangerous.

A very simple plate A has been cut out so that it will fit closely over wheel B and expose only the necessary amount of wheel at point E. You'll want to hinge one side so you can get the exact

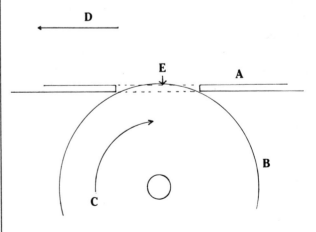

Figure 2-21

amount of exposed wheel you desire as well as compensate for wheel wear. Notice the rotation of the wheel C and where the operator stands, D, so that everything is moving *away* from the operator. Figure 2-22 shows the top view of our guard, and we can see the sides of our guard, F and G, help prevent the wheel from grabbing the tool. The thicker the sides F and G are, as shown by H, the less tool area we will have to make contact with our wheel if the tool has a handle, so H should be thick enough to be strong enough to prevent grabbing, but not too thick so as to prevent finishing the complete knife or tool blade.

The point of a tool will dig into a wheel quite easily, so be careful when you make contact with a wheel with the point of a knife, screwdriver, chisel, etc.

B contact would present less danger. And at point A, we can see that it is not possible for the wheel to grab the blade edge here, because the wheel surface is going away from the edge, not into it. In some cases, we do want the surface of the grinding wheel to go into the edge, as at point C. There is little doubt that a mechanical means to hold or contain the blade, along with caution and our protective equipment, is the way to go. Of course, contact with point C becomes more dangerous as the grinding wheel becomes softer, and absolutely impossible with rag wheels, felt wheels, rubber and leather wheels, and flap wheels. When using these, you must make contact with point A, and use the guard described in Figures 2-21 and 2-22.

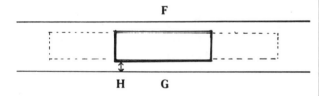

F

H   G

Figure 2-22

And the point of a tool will dig into the side of a grinding wheel, too, so be careful of that. This is one of the reasons we like to see grinding and sharpening machines going about 800 RPM or less.

And now let's talk about where we have to be especially careful when contacting a grinding wheel. In Figure 2-23, we have the same blade contacting a grinding wheel in three different places, A, B, and C. Notice center line E, and also clockwise wheel rotation D. Point C would be our most dangerous place to make contact with the wheel: a grab would throw the blade back into the operator, standing in direction F. Point

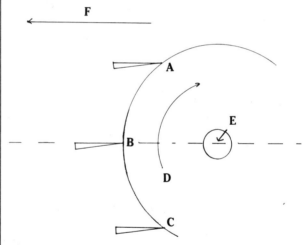

F

Figure 2-23

HANDLING A HONE

When you are sharpening an edge by hand, there are a number of ways to handle your hone, and they all seem to have their advantages as well as their disadvantages. As a minimum, we recommend using a hone at least 2″ × 6″, as anything smaller than this will be awkward to handle and will not allow you to get a full stroke of the edge.

One of the best and safest ways to use a hone is to place it on the edge of a bench top or desk. To prevent the hone from slipping around while you are grinding on it, you can either place it on a rubber pad or tack some small wood strips around it. Now you can get your fingers out of the way and the hone will remain stationary while you do your sharpening. Some people like to clamp their hone in a vise to do their sharpening (Picture 2-7), but you may have a hard time grinding all the way to the hilt of the blade when using this method.

Picture 2-7

A simple alternative would be to use Handi-Hones.* These are pressure-sensitive abrasives that can be placed on any flat surface. All you have to do is peel off the paper backing and stick them wherever is convenient. We have found that they produce an edge just as good if not better than any hone we have ever seen.

Another method is to hold the hone in your hand—but keep in mind this is much more dangerous and will require considerable care on your part. Because it is more dangerous, we do not recommend that anyone sharpen by holding a hone in their hands. But some of you are going to do it anyway, and at times it may be necessary, so you should be aware that there is a right way and a wrong way to do it. So let's study the correct way to handle a hone.

First, take your hand and fold back the three lower fingers, while pointing with the index finger. Then extend the thumb up, as in Picture 2-8. Remember when you were a kid and would make a pistol out of your hand and would run around shouting, "Bang, bang, I got you first"? Well, it's just about the same thing. Now place your hand on the hone and pick it up, as in Picture 2-9. Notice two things. First of all, the hone is always up on the ball of your thumb. Secondly, all your fingers are securely tucked *under* the surface of the hone (Picture 2-10), and anything peeking up over the surface will end up in a Band-Aid.

Always hold your work out from your body, and don't rest your arm or hand on your leg, but keep it well out in front of you (Picture 2-11). This will give you more of a feel for the edge, and will also be safer.

---

*Handi-Hones come in size 2″ × 6″ and are available from Razor Edge Systems, Inc., P.O. Box 150, Ely, MN 55731.

Picture 2-8

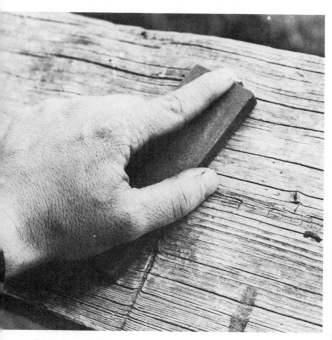

Picture 2-9

Picture 2-10

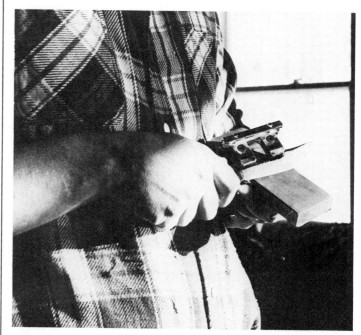

Picture 2-11

Notice how both of your hands can now get into the sharpening action. The hand holding the abrasive can "feel" the edge, and allow a better contact with less movement of the blade hand. The abrasive follows the entire edge as it moves across the surface (Pictures 2-12 and 2-13). We have found you will get better edges when the abrasive is held in the hand. This is because a lighter, more even stroke across the fine abrasive is possible, and consequently you get a better edge.

And let's not forget about safety. Whenever you are sharpening any edged tool, make sure that *all* of your actions are *always in superslow motion and very light!* Especially when you are just beginning. This is not just a safety factor; it allows you to study what you are doing—and move those pinkies before you whack one off.

Picture 2-12

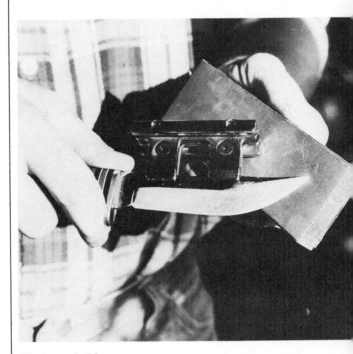

Picture 2-13

PART 2

SHARPENING THE SPORTSMAN'S TOOLS TO A RAZOR EDGE

So let's do a quick review and talk a little magic. *Abrasive, angle, technique.* The three magic words in sharpening. Use them all properly and you won't believe the results. If you goof with just one of them, you'll get nothing but frustration.

First let's tackle abrasives. We have learned that we must use abrasives at opposite ends of the scale—extremely coarse and extremely fine. But how do we tell what is coarse enough and what is fine enough? Well, the combination hones you can find in most any hardware store have one side that might be OK for your coarse grinding. Not that it couldn't be a little coarser, because it could. This is the hone you will use to remove all the scrap iron from your blade, of which there is usually plenty. Once that is accomplished you have to go to the other end of the rope to finish the edge. And how fine do you go? Just as fine as you can. It's not possible to go too fine. We have had hones made from optical flour and have still never seen a hone that is too fine. Now don't think that the fine side of that combination hone is fine enough, because it isn't. There is no such thing as a combination hone that will work as both a coarse and a fine, because they are virtually impossible to manufacture this way, unless you have two separate hones that have been glued together. The hard Arkansas stone will work all right, as will something like a fine barber's hone, and some ceramic hones. You can pretty well tell if a hone is fine enough by running your fingers across it. It should feel almost as smooth as glass. So in order to sharpen properly you must have one abrasive that is very coarse and one that is very fine. Without both you may as well forget sharpening.

Now let's get into angles. Seems like so many articles have been written telling us that we must use a certain precise angle when sharpening a particular blade. To that we say *bunk!* You can use any angle you wish, just so you finish under 25°. Now let's not confuse sharpening angle with relief angle. The relief angle is the angle we use to taper the blade back to the proper thickness *directly behind the cutting edge.* The sharpening angle deals only with the first 1/32″, or even less, depending on how well we have tapered back our relief. In Figure II-1 you can see the angles we are concerned with. In A, we are grinding in relief, and can either lay the blade flat on the abrasive, which will give a better relief, or we can use a slight clearance angle. Then when we go to the finishing abrasive we increase the grinding angle, but never over 25°, as shown in B. This is true for both double bevel and single bevel blades, but remember, we *never* touch an abrasive to the flat side of a single bevel blade unless it is parallel to the blade, and then *only* with a fine abrasive. If you use too little angle, you are forgiven, because you can always increase it. But if you use too much angle to begin with you will ruin your edge and end up back at square one.

25° OR LESS

A   B

Figure II-1

And last, but certainly not least, we must use proper technique. For the coarse grinding you can use most any grinding motion. It can be back and forth, clockwise, or counterclockwise. Most people prefer a circular motion, but use whatever suits you best. That is on the coarse abrasive; when you go to the fine abrasive, it's another story. Here you have to be more fussy.

The finishing stroke must always be *into* the cutting edge, as shown in Figure II-2. Do this stroke in superslow motion so that you can closely watch the edge contact the abrasive. If you have a curved blade you will have to be raising the handle through the stroke so that the entire edge wipes the abrasive. When you have this stroke mastered on both sides, you *only use alternate* strokes to finish the edge. This means one stroke on one side and one on the other.

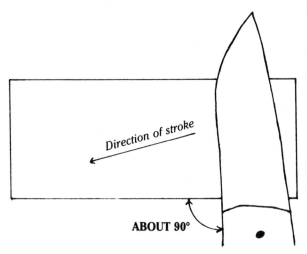

Figure II-2

After a dozen or so of the alternate strokes you will feel the edge become smoother. As you finish, use very light strokes. The last few strokes on the fine abrasive should be just the weight of the knife.

Abrasive, angle, technique. If you understand and properly use all three of these, you are on your way to producing the best edges ever.

What You'll Need

There are many products and devices on the market for sharpening tools. Many are expensive, and some are useless. With the simplest equipment listed below you'll have all you'll need to put a razor-sharp edge on any tool.

1. A FAST-CUTTING ABRASIVE. Since you always begin by tapering back the blade, you'll need an abrasive that is capable of rapidly cutting away the excess steel. There are a number of abrasives you can use for this purpose:

Grinding wheel. A fine grinding wheel is comparable to a very coarse sharpening stone. Look for the marking of grit size. #36 is very coarse; #60 is coarse; #100 is fine. You want #100. Take a piece of hard steel or an old knife to test it out. If the wheel cuts rapidly and doesn't leave furrows which are too deep, it's just about right.

Sanding disk. The kind you want is used for auto body and fender work. Look on the fiber side for the grit number. Again, a grit size of about #100 will be OK. Remember though, disks, like all coated abrasives, get dull with use. A used disk marked #100 will cut like a finer grade abrasive as it wears out.

Coarse hone. Usually this comes as a combination hone. The coarse side is suitable for blade tapering, then the finer side will give you a little smoother finish. The smoother you go, the finer abrasive you'll need. And if you are a professional, you'll want a *very* smooth blade because this reduces face friction, and your hand, wrist, and arm will feel a lot better at the end of your eight-hour day.

2. A FINISHING ABRASIVE. The hone you buy should be at least five inches long and two inches wide, especially if you are using a guide for sharpening. It's just too awkward using anything smaller. A ceramic hone or a good hard Arkansas is good for finishing, as are some of the very fine manufactured hones. As for grit size, look for #400 or finer. Fine hones come in grit sizes all the way down to #1,000 or finer, but they're expensive and you don't need more than a #400 to #600 plus your sharpening steel to get a great edge.

3. AN EDGE GUIDE. You can get a good usable edge by sharpening free hand, but there is no way even a professional can match a novice using a guide. This simple mechanical device assures a constant correct angle, and removes much of the frustration of sharpening.

4. A SHARPENING STEEL. After the fine abrasive, you will want a sharpening steel to achieve the ultimate edge. There are many steels of all shapes and textures on the market. Unfortunately, except for a very few available to the professional sharpener, they are all rough as a cob and consequently useless. All you'll do is tear up the fine edge you so carefully put on with the finest abrasive you could find. So if you can't see your face reflected in the steel that touches your blade, forget it. The shape of the steeling tool is not too important, but it should provide some method of indicating the proper angle.

You now have all the equipment you need for sharpening—but there is just one more thing. How can you tell when the blade is sharp?

5. AN EDGE TESTER. Without some way of testing your edge, you just don't know when to stop. An Edge Tester will do the trick here, whether your tool is a knife, an ice auger, an ax, or even a fishhook. It solves one of the oldest problems in sharpening, and it will never tell you a fib.

If there's one thing most people want to know how to sharpen really well, it's the knife. Knives come in all sizes and shapes, and some are designed for special-purpose cutting, but the way you sharpen to get a really keen edge remains pretty much the same. We'll use as our example the most popular knife of the sportsman, the jackknife.

The jackknife is easy to carry and is long enough to do the trick for most any job you might want to do in the field. In fact, there is no reason why you can't completely butcher your game with one of the larger jackknives. In the packing industry the most popular blade length is six inches, and many shorter blades are used. Sometimes they process bulls that go close to a ton and a half, so if you have a good-sized folding knife, you should have plenty of knife to do the job.

The knife we are using for this demonstration is the one we found out near the barn in a pile of manure, and as you can see, it is almost as good as new. If it had been made of high carbon steel, we would have had just a piece of rust, like the wrench that was found with it. Look at the blade and the cutting edge (Picture 3-1) and you can see that this knife suffered from the same fate that most knives do: its owner sharpened only on the cutting edge, and didn't taper the blade back a little with each sharpening to improve that all-important relief. Maybe he just wanted to keep the pretty picture on the blade, but he had two choices. He could either keep the pretty picture and have a dull blade, or he could forget the picture and have a sharp blade.

Figure 3-1 clearly illustrates what happens when a blade is not tapered back each time it is sharpened. This is one of the big sins in sharpening, and it is almost always done. Normally the sportsman starts out with a properly tapered blade, similar to angle ABC. As he sharpens his

CHAPTER 3
Sharpening the Folding Knife

Picture 3-1

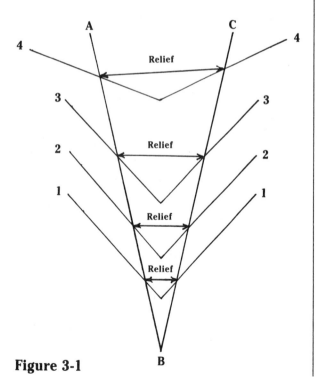

Figure 3-1

knife he doesn't bother to taper the blade back, and the relief gets progressively thicker. As the relief gets thicker, the knife gets harder and harder to sharpen, and finally he reaches a point where the edge is so thick and blunt that he has a hard time putting even a poor edge on his knife. He ends up in total frustration and wonders why.

The very first thing we do with a knife is check its relief. Always. To do this, put the blade between your thumb and finger and slowly move the blade out, noting how thick or thin it feels (Picture 3-2). If the relief of your blade is good, you will hardly feel the cutting edge separate your fingers and it will feel as though there is no change in the surface, that it is flat. On the other hand, if the blade has a poor relief it will feel thick right behind the cutting edge, as if you were running a piece of blunt metal or wire between your fingers. Experience will make you better at this, but once you get used to it you'll find it a very handy method of determining the relief of a blade.

So the first thing we must do with this knife is correct the poor relief. To taper the blade back, lay it flat on the surface of your coarse abrasive (Picture 3-3), lift the back of the blade just enough to give a slight clearance angle, and then begin scrubbing the blade in. You will get a clear picture of what we are doing by looking at Figure 3-2. The less clearance angle you use, the better your edge will turn out, but it will also take more time to grind in your burr.

Stop grinding periodically and check your blade to see how you are doing. A magnifying glass will be handy for this if you have one (Picture 3-4). Notice how the grind marks, or furrows, start back away from the cutting edge; as you continue grinding they progress toward the edge, as shown in Figure 3-3. When the furrows finally reach the cutting edge, your burr will begin to form, as shown in Figure 3-4. When you feel a

Abrasive

Figure 3-2

Picture 3-2

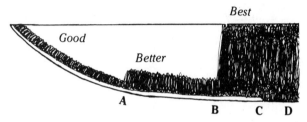

Figure 3-3 *Here we have a drawing of our jackknife blade, and notice how there are three different clearance angles indicated. From the tip of the blade to point A, the furrows extend just a short distance up the blade, indicating a steep grinding angle. From point A to point B we have decreased the clearance angle, as the furrows extend farther up the blade. The area from point B to point C indicates that we have the blade flat on the hone with no clearance angle, which will give us the best results. Notice that none of the furrows extends all the way to the edge as yet; we have to continue grinding, and gradually the furrows will reach the cutting edge. At point D the furrow marks reach the edge, and the burr will begin to form, telling us to stop grinding on this side. Remember, the less clearance angle we use, the better our final edge will be.*

Picture 3-3

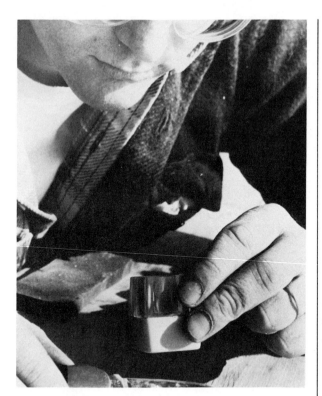

Picture 3-4

Picture 3-5

The burr is always turned UP from the abrasive

O CLEARANCE
ANGLE

Figure 3-4

good burr running the entire length of the edge (Picture 3-5), you can stop grinding.

The farther the furrows extend up the edge, the better the relief will be, and the better the final edge will be. In Picture 3-6 you can see that we have ground most of our pretty picture from the knife, but it is more than worth it to have a superb edge on the blade.

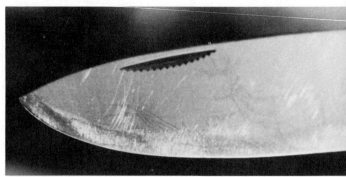

Picture 3-6

Once we grind in a good burr, we flip the blade over and scrub the other side in the same way. As we've said, most people prefer a circular scrubbing motion, but it doesn't really matter as long as you get the job done, so suit yourself. When the furrow marks extend all the way to the edge, begin checking for the burr. You can also use an Edge Tester for this purpose, as shown in Picture 3-7. Remember, the burr is always turned *up*, so be sure you're checking the side that was *away* from the abrasive. This is important, because you'll just scrub your blade away if you are checking the wrong side for a burr!

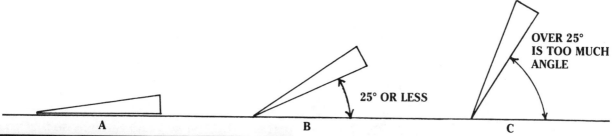

25° OR LESS

OVER 25°
IS TOO MUCH
ANGLE

A   B   C

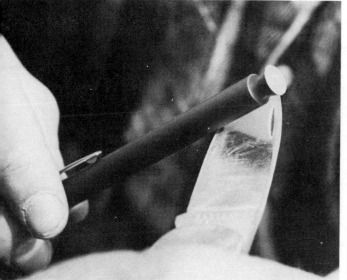

Picture 3-7

Figure 3-5 *Here you can clearly see the angles we are using to sharpen our jackknife. The angle in A is what we used to grind in a burr on the coarse abrasive. We laid the blade flat on the abrasive, although you could use a slight clearance angle to grind in your burr; however, the flatter you lay the blade, the better your relief and final edge will be. When you go to the fine abrasive, you increase the angle to 25° or less, as in B. If you use too great an angle, as in C, you will ruin your edge and will have to start all over from scratch.*

Once we have run a burr on both sides of the blade we are ready to go to the fine abrasive to finish the edge. In this case we are using a fine-coated abrasive, which we have found to be excellent for fine honing. Now we increase the angle slightly over what we used to grind in the burr, as shown in Figure 3-5, and our stroke should always be *into* the cutting edge, as in Figure 3-6. We begin the stroke at the heel of the blade (Picture 3-8), and as we draw the edge across the abrasive we lift the handle (Picture 3-9) so that at the end of the stroke we should

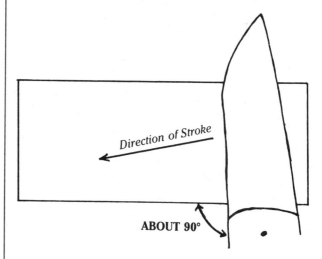

Direction of Stroke

ABOUT 90°

Figure 3-6

Picture 3-8

be way out on the tip of the blade (Picture 3-10). Make this stroke in very slow motion, always *into* the cutting edge, and study it carefully, making sure that the entire edge has wiped the abrasive. Then do the same stroke on the other side (Pictures 3-11 to 3-13).

Now practice this stroke until you are an expert at it. Do it slowly and carefully so that you can study what you are doing, and don't hurry your blade off the abrasive at the end of the stroke. This is a common mistake that ruins the tip—the most important part of your blade. In butchering you'll use the first two inches of the blade most of the time, and many butchers are happy if they can just keep the end of their blade sharp. But, of course, we would never be happy with this, as we must have our whole blade perfect!

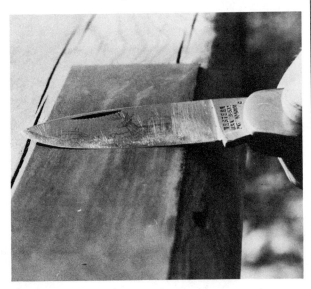

Picture 3-9

Picture 3-10

Picture 3-11

Picture 3-12

Picture 3-13

When you have this stroke mastered on both sides, then use only *alternate* strokes, one on one side and one on the other. Do this a dozen times or so, and then do a few very light and slow strokes. Now test your edge (Pictures 3-14 and 3-15), and if it doesn't check out to be perfect try another half dozen alternate strokes. You might like to study what you're doing to the edge with a magnifying glass.

Remember to try to keep a constant angle throughout the stroke and make sure the entire

Picture 3-14

Picture 3-15

edge wipes the abrasive. Use slow-motion strokes so you can study what you're doing, and make sure the last few strokes on the fine abrasive are very light—just the weight of the knife.

Let's see how well we have done on this edge and try to shave with it. In Picture 3-16 you can see the hairs popping off the arm like nobody's business. If your edge didn't turn out quite this good don't let it bother you. Do some more practicing and pretty soon you'll be able to consistently turn out edges that will make your hunting partner green with envy.

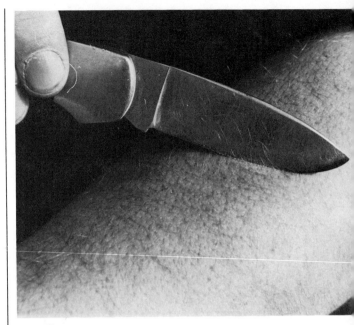

Picture 3-16

Now we are going to sharpen the folding knife again, but this time we are going to use a guide, which will be a great help. Sharpening free-handed and sharpening with a guide are two completely different things. You have to remember that when we're talking about an edge, we're talking about something that is microscopic, and trying to find it by hand is just an impossible task. This doesn't mean that you can't get an excellent edge by hand, because the last chapter just proved that you can. But if you're looking for the absolute ultimate in an edge, you will never get it using the free-handed method.

First of all, sharpening is very simple when you're using a guide, because it provides you with precise control as well as proper angle. Of course, it is important to understand the manufacturer's instructions thoroughly, so go over them carefully. Everything is built right into the tool, and using the guide is an almost foolproof method of sharpening. The best thing about using the sharpening guide is the result. There is just no comparison between the results you get when using a guide and sharpening free-handed, as you will see.

In Picture 4-1 we are loading the knife into the sharpening guide. If you are right-handed, hold the guide in the left hand with the screw heads facing upward so that they can be tightened. The guide rests in the palm of your hand, while the forefinger and thumb grasp the knife blade, allowing you to tighten the guide with your free hand.

Ordinarily the first thing we would do is taper the relief back a little farther, but we did such a good job with it in the last chapter we can go right to sharpening. The farther back the guide is mounted on the blade, the less the grinding angle will be, so we have mounted the guide as far back on the blade as we can get it.

CHAPTER 4

Sharpening the Folding Knife with the Aid of a Sharpening Guide

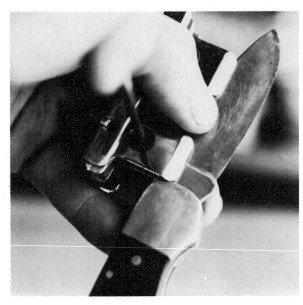

Picture 4-1

In Figure 4-1 we have a diagram of what your edge might look like. The angles in the drawing are slightly exaggerated so you can get the idea. The first thing we always do is check the relief of a blade. A blade with good relief might look something like angle ABC. Once you have the proper relief, you are ready to grind in the secondary edge faces DF and DG. To do this we go to the coarse hone and begin grinding until we run that burr the entire length of the edge (Pictures 4-2 and 4-3).

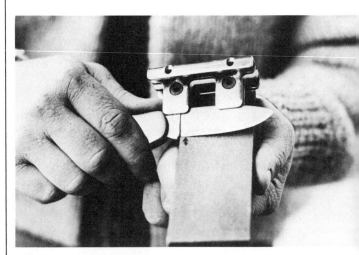

Picture 4-2

After properly mounting the Razor Edge on your blade, begin grinding on the coarse hone in a circular motion. Grind until a burr can be felt along the entire edge of the opposite side of the blade. IT IS MOST IMPORTANT THAT A BURR RUN THE ENTIRE LENGTH OF THE BLADE! When you get the burr, repeat on the other side of the blade until a burr is felt.

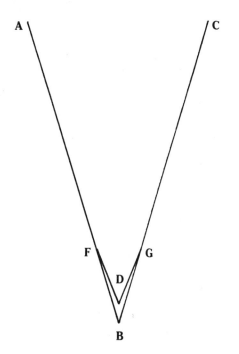

Secondary edge faces are indicated by DF and DG.

Figure 4-1

When you are using a sharpening guide, it is important always to place the guide on the abrasive first, and then drop the edge down to do your grinding. If you touch the edge to the abrasive before the guide, chances are you will

Picture 4-3

Picture 4-4

have our secondary edge faces as shown in Figure 4-3. They are only about 1/32″ wide, which tells a lot about our relief. The better the relief of the blade, the thinner the secondary edge face will be. You will also notice that with better relief your burr will come up quicker, and your final edge will be better, too. Now you can see just how big a role relief plays in sharpening.

Now that we have ground a burr on both sides of the blade, we are ready to go to the fine abrasive. We will increase our angle slightly, as shown in Figure 4-2, by moving the blade back into the sharpening guide about 1/8″. When we go from the coarse abrasive to the fine, we increase from angle A to angle B. This is double-edging, and when we are finished, the final edge will look like angle EGH in Figure 4-3. Of course, the angles in the diagrams are exaggerated to

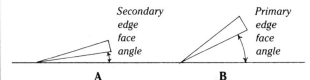

Figure 4-2

ruin the edge, and this is even more critical on the finishing abrasive.

After just a little grinding our burr popped right up. This is an indication of very good relief. The better your relief, the less grinding you have to do to get that burr. This burr is so strong that it is easily visible in Picture 4-4. Now we flip the blade over and run a burr all along the other side. Again the burr pops up right away, and we can expect a superb edge when we are finished.

In examining what we have done to the edge so far, we can see that because we are using a sharpening guide our grinding appears very flat and uniform on both sides of the edge. We now

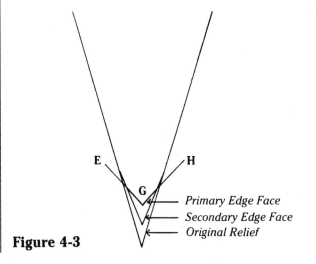

Figure 4-3

give you a clearer idea of what we are doing, but GE and GH will be the primary edge faces, which do the actual cutting.

As we said before, when you are finishing your edge on the fine abrasive it is *very important* always to touch the sharpening guide to the abrasive first, and then the cutting edge. If you touch the edge to the abrasive before the guide you will ruin your edge. Also make sure that throughout the finishing stroke the sharpening guide remains in contact with the abrasive at all times. If you lift the guide while the edge maintains contact, you will ruin your edge this way as well.

Start at the heel of the blade and draw it across the abrasive, making sure that the entire edge wipes the abrasive through the stroke (Pictures 4-5 and 4-6). Do about a dozen alternate strokes, and remember, the last few strokes on the fine abrasive are always very, very light.

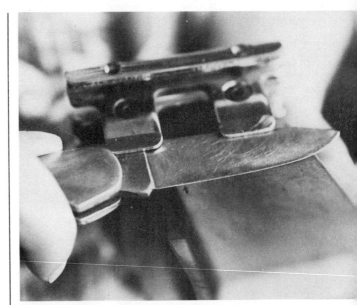

Picture 4-5

Picture 4-6

A quick check of the edge feels very good (Picture 4-7), and it makes an excellent shaving edge (Picture 4-8). It effortlessly pops the hair from the arm. You will readily notice a huge difference between an edge that is sharpened free-handed and one that is sharpened by using a guide. There is just no comparison.

Picture 4-7

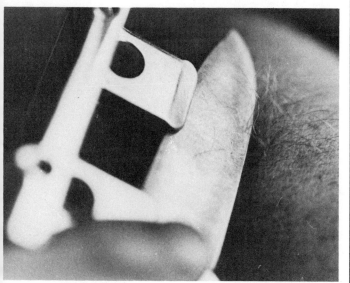

Picture 4-8

CHAPTER 5

Sharpening the Ax

One of the most puzzling of all tools to sharpen is also one of the easiest to sharpen, but you surely would never know it by studying some of the axes around our town of Ely. Ely is called the canoe capital of the world, and it's probably the dull ax capital, too. You see, people come from all parts of the world to go canoeing up here, and one of the tools the local outfitters supply to these tourists is an ax. We don't just have wilderness, we also have rock formations as hard as any in the world, and as one old guide said, "Everybody cuts and splits their camp wood on solid granite." Are you beginning to suspect the problem? Once the edge of that ax strikes the granite, it's all done, and it seems that happens just about every other stroke. If you are looking for frustrated ax sharpeners, you're sure to find them up here. When you use an ax, always make sure that when your stroke misses the wood or goes all the way through it, your edge will just bury itself in a wood block, and not in the ground, and certainly not in a rock!

We have chosen a double-bladed ax for our sharpening demonstration. In Picture 5-1 you can see that the edge shows signs of abuse, but fortunately not the granite type. Before we start sharpening, look at Picture 5-2 to see the effects of this dull edge when cutting into an aspen tree. You can see that in striking the tree the ax had no control. It skidded dangerously in the path of least resistance because there was no edge to guide it. Poor edge relief has added to this problem and caused a bouncing action, resulting in the curved cut. The ax did not actually cut the aspen, but sheared the chip out, as you can see by the rough edges.

Just for the heck of it, let's check the primary edge face angle on this ax before we sharpen it to see what we can learn (Pictures 5-3 and 5-4). As best as we can determine, we come up

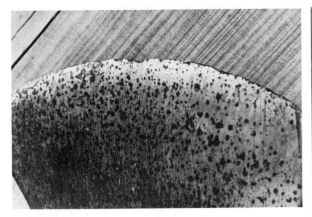

Picture 5-1

Picture 5-2

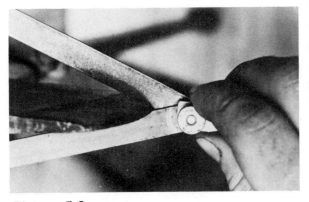

Picture 5-3

with a whopping 40°. What a billy club! No wonder it just hacked that chip out of our aspen.

Now we'll take the ax to the hollow grinder and get started with the sharpening. First we take a "printout" to see where the grinding wheel is contacting our blade (Picture 5-5). Our first "print" is rather close to the edge, and we want a good relief, so we'll move the base of our guide *toward* the grinding wheel. This will put the contact point with the grinding wheel farther back from the edge. Another print shows that we are still too close to the edge, so we again move our guide *toward* the grinding wheel and try again. This time our print looks OK, so we'll leave the guide where it is (Picture 5-6).

Now let's grind in a nice hollow grind all along the blade edge, and yep, you guessed it, we have quite a little grinding to do to get all those nasty nicks out of the edge. You wouldn't want anyone to catch you with even a little nick in your ax, now would you? Also, you'll want to keep a bucket of water handy so your blade doesn't get too hot. This is more important as the edge gets thinner because there isn't as much metal to absorb the heat.

Before we go all the way down with our hollow grind, we'll true up the edge and get all the nicks out of it (Pictures 5-7 and 5-8). Just put the ax perpendicular to the grinding wheel, then *slowly* and easily grind in the contour of the edge you want, at the same time removing the nicks.

Now continue your hollow grinding until you get a burr running the entire length of the edge (Picture 5-9). When you reach this point, flip your blade over and grind on the other side until you get that burr, and we will then have a good relief on our ax.

Relief on an ax is important, but it is possible to have too much relief. For instance, when you are cutting into a log, once the fibers have been

Picture 5-4

Picture 5-7

Picture 5-5

Picture 5-8

Picture 5-6

Picture 5-9

cut the blade should "kick" the chip out. If your ax has too much relief, the wood chips will stay in place and you can whack away all day long and not get anywhere. It is the wedging action of your ax blade that kicks the chips out, allowing you to continue cutting. So it is better to have not enough relief on your ax than too much, because you can always grind it down more.

When you compare an ax to a knife, you can understand why one should have more relief than the other. The knife is a slashing tool and the ax is a striking tool, so the edge on the ax must be more durable to withstand the shock of the blow. This is especially true when chopping hardwoods, and more so with hardwood knots. You might end up with too much relief, as you'll find out when you chop into a hardwood knot, especially if it's frozen. If you end up with visible damage to your edge, you know you have ground in too much relief, but the only way to find this point is by experience, and your preference will depend on how you use your ax.

Look at Figure 5-1 and you can see the difference between the original relief on our ax,

and the relief we just ground in. Bear in mind that this drawing was made to bring out a point rather than be accurate, but we tried to be accurate, too. Look at the difference in the edge at point A. It's no wonder that our penetration was so poor. It's surprising that the ax didn't just bounce back at us. Look at the pressure arrows on the right stroke, and you can see what caused the blade to turn as it struck the wood, giving it that "glancing" feeling. The edge was too dull to keep penetrating so it just turned to the left.

Now that we have run a burr on each side of our ax with the hollow grinder, giving us good relief, we are ready to do our actual sharpening. All of the grinding we have done so far has been only for the relief of the ax, which you need in order to put on a good edge.

First we go to the coarse abrasive, and with the hollow grind burr facing downward, we hold the ax at an angle slightly greater than that of the hollow grind (Picture 5-10) and grind in our secondary edge face. When you get your burr flip the blade over and do the same on the other

Figure 5-1

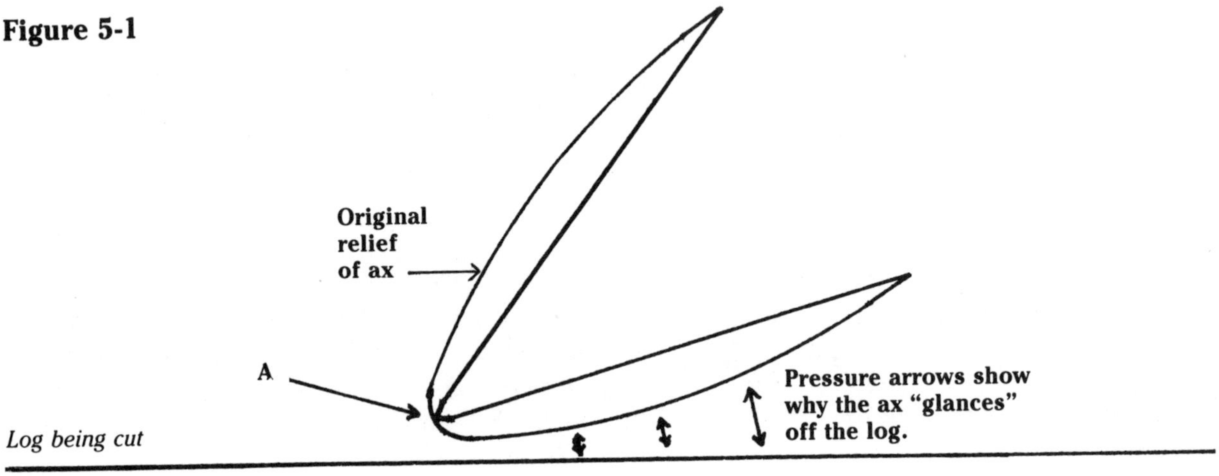

Original
relief
of ax →

A →

Log being cut

Pressure arrows show
why the ax "glances"
off the log.

Picture 5-10

Picture 5-11

Picture 5-12

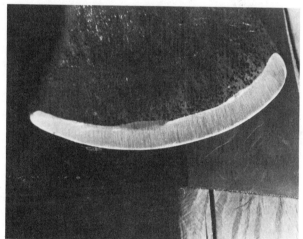

Picture 5-13

side. When you have ground in a burr on both sides, your secondary edge angle is finished, and you are ready to go to the fine abrasive.

Again, we increase the angle slightly to give us our primary edge face. Beginning at the heel of the edge (Picture 5-11), draw the edge across the abrasive (Picture 5-12), and by the end of your stroke you should be well up on the toe of

the blade (Picture 5-13). You should practice this stroke on one side until you have it mastered, then practice the same stroke on the other side of the blade. Always use a slow, careful action, and study how the edge contacts the abrasive as you draw it across. Practice this on both sides until you are proficient at it, and from then on use all alternate strokes, once on one

Picture 5-14

Picture 5-15

side and once on the other. Try about a dozen alternate strokes and then check your edge to see what you have (Picture 5-14).

Hmm, our edge still feels a little rough. We try another dozen or so of the alternate strokes and test the edge again. This time it feels terrific.

Let's check our edge angle again to see what we have now (Picture 5-15). Our check shows that we have slightly under 25°, which is a big difference from the 40° we had originally. Let's go see what happens in our aspen log now.

The difference is astounding. In Picture 5-16 you can see that the cut was not deflected as before, but sliced into the wood. Instead of being concave the cuts are now straight, and are very smooth to the touch. Our relief seems just about right, as it did a good job of kicking the chips out of the cut. Now that this ax has a good edge on it, it is much easier and much safer to use than it was before.

Now for the real test: we'll go to some dry, hard tamarack to see what happens. If we have created an edge that won't kick the chip or won't stand up in this hardwood, we have not done a very good job.

Picture 5-16

We abusively chop away at some of the very hard knots in the dry tamarack, and afterward we find the edge to be excellent. It wasn't chipped out or turned over, and it was still very sharp. We did a good job in our sharpening.

Now, just for the sake of experimenting, we are going to take a hammer and tap a small imperfection into the edge of our ax, and see what effect this has when we cut into the aspen. In Picture 5-17 you can notice the rough imperfection in the wood. This is where we put the nick in the blade; the wood wasn't actually cut, but was torn apart by the force of the blade. This is what the whole edge was doing before we sharpened it.

There is much to sharpening an ax, especially if you're the kind of guy who has to have the best. Someday we'll go into the fine-tuning of an ax, much the same as if we were going to use it in competition This will probably be a whole new subject in another book. For general cutting purposes, what you have learned here will be plenty, and we wish you luck as you put your first real edge on your ax.

Picture 5-17

CHAPTER 6
Sharpening Plane Blades

If ever the woodworker had a problem with one of his tools, it was with his plane. We have seen more frustrated woodworkers with plane in hand and hopeless look on face, so we are going to help you iron out this problem right now. Plane blades are no big deal, and we just need a little understanding of what a plane is all about. First of all, what kind of edge do we have? Yep, we're talking about the single bevel blade, and the most important thing we can remember about this blade is that we *never* grind metal from the straight side of the edge.

We bought a brand-new small plane to use for this lesson just to see what we might learn. The package it came in promised us a "smooth cutting blade," but when we took it apart and tested the edge (Picture 6-1), our Edge Tester told us that promise was going to be broken, and the surface of the pine we planed with the factory edge was very rough. Another indicator of a poor edge is the way the wood fibers hang up on the blade (Picture 6-2). We are not cutting the wood, but are tearing it apart, and this blade obviously needs help—lots of it!

A very common mistake in using a plane is loading the blade the wrong way. In Figures 6-1 and 6-2, you can see the difference when the same blade is loaded differently. The dotted lines indicate the center of the edge angle; notice in Figure 6-1 the angle is a whopping 40° to the cutting plane, while in 6-2 we have a more pleasant 22°. It's not difficult to see that the blade in Figure 6-2 is going to cut much better than the blade in Figure 6-1. As a matter of fact, if we stood the blade in 6-1 up any farther, it probably wouldn't even cut at all! Also, the blade in 6-2 will tend to produce nice, long, curled wood shavings, while the blade in 6-1 will probably produce short chips.

Also important, as shown in Figure 6-2, we must have sufficient clearances at points C and

Picture 6-1

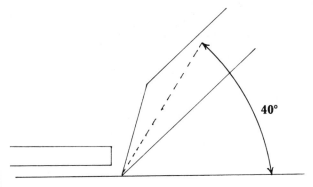

Figure 6-1

Picture 6-2

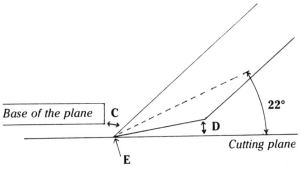

Figure 6-2

D. If the heel of the blade at point D is riding on the wood, the cutting edge at point E will be sitting up in the breeze where it is no good to anyone. And if we don't have proper clearance at point C, the wood shavings will clog up and create more problems.

Just like most other tools, most plane blades are also built with a poor relief. The blade we have here has an edge angle of about 30°, but it should be between 20° and 25°, so this is the first thing we will take care of. It would be much easier and quicker if we were to go out and do this on the hollow grinder, but this is a fairly small blade and shouldn't take us too long to grind by hand. We are going to use a guide on this blade, and we can expect something spectacular when we are finished. We mount the guide about 3/4 of an inch back from the edge (Picture 6-3), and then we grind, and we grind, and we grind some more. Right now we're wishing that we had gone out to use the hollow grinder, but we grind just a little bit more and our relief will be OK. In Figure 6-3, you can see how we had to grind down the heel of the blade at point C until we had what looks like line AB. Now that

Picture 6-3

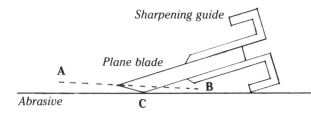

Figure 6-3

we have ground in our relief, we are ready to grind in an edge.

First we have to increase our grinding angle a few degrees by running the plane blade up into the guide about 1/8 of an inch. Then we go back to the coarse abrasive and grind in a good strong burr across the entire edge. Remember, on a single bevel blade, we *grind only on one side!* As soon as we get a good burr, we again move our guide to increase the grinding angle a few more degrees, and then we go to the fine abrasive.

Now if this seems a little confusing, remember that the reason we have increased our angle twice is because we used the sharpening guide to grind in the relief on the blade. If we had used the hollow grinder to get our relief, then we would just have mounted the blade in the guide, scrubbed in a burr, and then we would have increased the grinding angle only once before going to the fine abrasive.

Now remember, it is very important that we grind a burr *only on one side on a single bevel blade.* In Figure 6-4 you can see the various angles we have used throughout the sharpening process. In A we are grinding in relief until the total edge angle is 25° or less. Then we increase the grinding angle, as in B, and grind in a good strong burr, and this is our secondary edge face. Now we increase the angle again, as in C, and go to the fine abrasive, and this gives us our primary edge face. The only time we touch an abrasive to the straight side of the blade is to remove the burr. This must be done *only on the fine abrasive,* and you must *always hold the blade flat on the abrasive,* as shown in Picture 6-4D.

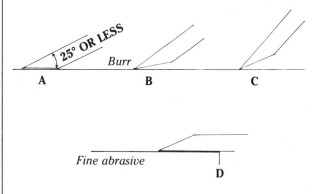

Figure 6-4

So let's go to the fine abrasive and take about a dozen strokes (Picture 6-4). (The strokes may be taken in any direction.) Then turn the blade over, making certain it is lying flat on the abrasive (Picture 6-5), and take another dozen strokes. Now we'll take a few alternate strokes, one on one side and one on the other. We test the edge (Picture 6-6), and it doesn't feel quite up to snuff, so we go back to the fine abrasive for another dozen or so of the alternate strokes. This time the test tells us we can smile.

We'll take nothing for granted, though, so we'll test the plane on the pine board again. With a sharp blade there is a considerable difference.

Picture 6-4

Picture 6-5

The planed surface is smooth, and we no longer have wood fibers hanging up on the cutting edge.

For a more crucial test, let's see what the plane will do to a piece of leather. As you can see by the curl in Picture 6-7, the plane blade is cutting the tough leather rather easily. If you have gotten an edge on your plane blade that cuts leather this easily, you will be tickled pink by the planing results on your next wood project.

Picture 6-6

Picture 6-7

Seems like few hunters really understand the arrowhead. Many don't realize that their arrowheads should be sharpened, or just how important it is that they be kept razor-sharp. Some hunters aren't even sure what kind of arrowheads they should be using, for that matter, so let's try to draw a bead on some of these points.

First, let's try to determine how to choose the best arrowhead for the job. The most important consideration is what we call the slash factor. To understand this, we have to understand how an arrow kills. When you hunt with a rifle, you have to consider things like the size of your bullet and its speed, because a rifle kills by shock. But an arrow is different. Sometimes you'll hear a bowhunter say that his deer didn't even know it was hit, and then after a period of time it just dropped over. That is because an arrow kills by causing an animal to bleed to death. So the most desirable arrowhead is the one that will cause the most bleeding, which makes the slash factor easier to understand. It is simply the amount of flesh that the arrowhead will cut and leave bleeding as it passes through.

In Figure 7-1 you can see how the slash factor is measured. We have to depend on this cut to provide sufficient bleeding to result in death, so the greater the slash factor of the arrowhead, the faster the animal will bleed to death. Now you can see how important the slash factor is in determining what arrowhead design you are going to use.

And how do we determine the slash factor of an arrowhead? Well, there are different ways of measuring the different types of arrowheads, but it is basically quite simple. On a simple broadhead, where the two cutting edges meet at the point and lie in the same plane, you must measure the greatest distance between the edges, as shown in Figure 7-1. However, measuring the slash

CHAPTER 7

Sharpening Arrowheads

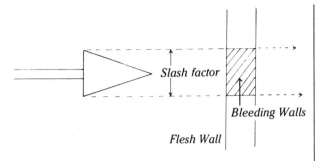

Figure 7-1

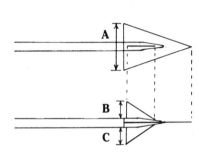

On a broadhead, where two edges meet at the tip and are on the same plane, you measure the greatest distance between the edges.

The slash factor on an insert blade is measured only from the tip of the edge to the ferrule.

Figure 7-2

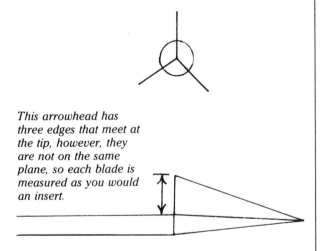

This arrowhead has three edges that meet at the tip, however, they are not on the same plane, so each blade is measured as you would an insert.

Figure 7-3

factor of an insert blade is quite different, as you can see in Figure 7-2. Here we measure from the tip of the insert edge to the base of the ferrule, as shown by B and C. Remember, if two edges are on the same plane and meet at the tip, you just measure the greatest distance between the edges, so the total slash factor of the arrowhead in Figure 7-2 would be A plus B plus C.

In Figure 7-3 we have a three-bladed arrowhead. All three edges do meet at the tip, but they are *not* on the same plane, so you measure this type of blade just as you would an insert, and multiply by three, because all three blades are the same.

If an insert is located farther up on the arrowhead, as shown in Figure 7-4, you measure much the same as if it were mounted on the ferrule. You measure from the highest point of the insert to the base, but as with the insert mounted on the ferrule, *do not* include the base it is mounted on, which in this case is the thickness of the broadhead. So the total slash factor of the arrowhead in Figure 7-4 would be the sum of distances A, B, and C.

If we were to shoot just a pointed target arrow into an animal, we would have a very ineffective wound, because the point will just force the flesh apart enough to allow the arrow to pass through. If the arrow passes all the way through the animal, the wound will close behind it with very little bleeding; however, chances are this arrow will remain in the wound, blocking off any bleeding. It is the slash factor that causes the animal to bleed, and the slash factor on a target arrow is just about zero.

In Figure 7-5, look at the big difference in the slash factor between the broadhead in A, and the insert type blade in B. Notice in A how the blade has opened up an entire flesh wall so that the whole arrow can slip effortlessly through the wound. There is very little resistance against the

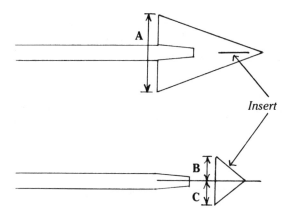

Figure 7-4

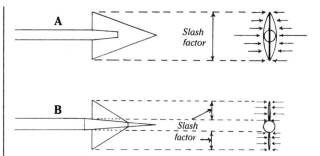

Figure 7-5

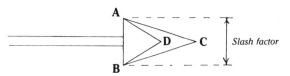

Figure 7-6

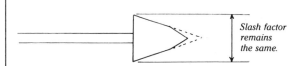

Figure 7-7

ferrule and shaft, and this wound should bleed profusely. The arrowhead in B has much less of a slash factor, and notice how the shaft of the arrow has to squeeze through the flesh, much like the target arrow. Much of this wound will close as the arrow passes through, and it will cause much less bleeding than the wound in A.

Why not run your own little slash factor test. When the wife isn't looking, swipe one of her synthetic sponges. Soak it in warm water and then stand it up and run an arrow through it. This way you can see and study for yourself the different effects of different arrowheads. Just don't forget to put the sponge back when you are finished. (She'll never know the difference.)

So don't be too impressed with the great claims and designs of arrowheads. It seems that most of them are made either to look or sound deadly, or both, but it all boils down to one thing—slash factor.

In Figure 7-6 you can also see that the length of the cutting edge is not that critical. An arrowhead shaped like ACB has no more of a slash factor than an arrowhead like ADB. One thing you have to be careful of with long, narrow blades is a weak tip, especially with the compound bows

we have today. Regardless of design, no arrowhead is going to withstand hitting something very hard without sustaining some damage, so we have to be concerned about a strong tip. After all, if the tip doesn't penetrate, nothing behind it will either.

In Picture 7-1 you can see two arrowheads. One is OK, but the other has a bent tip, which first of all will not penetrate very well, and secondly will produce poor quality bleeding walls. Any tip that is bent or seems weak should be shortened, as shown in Figure 7-7. You can see that the slash factor will remain the same, but you will end up with a more dependable tip on your arrowhead. Now if we could hunt animals that had no bones, a long, narrow tip would be more desirable because it will penetrate a little better, but until someone starts making game animals with boneless shoulders, we will have to take for granted that we aren't going to be so lucky as to make a bone-free shot.

Now let's talk about why an arrowhead should be absolutely razor-sharp. We haven't had any arrows shot at us lately, but we can perhaps best explain this by telling you some experiences we have had in cutting ourselves. (Purely unintentional!)

The sharpening machines we build for the packing industry are made of stainless steel. These stainless steel sheets are cut to size in a large shear, which leaves a rough, ragged burr on the edge. Sometimes while handling these sheets of steel, we cut ourselves on that burr, and we noticed that these cuts didn't bleed much, but they did take a long time to heal. This cut was the result of a dull, ragged edge. But sometimes we cut ourselves with a very smooth, sharp edge, too. In a packing plant when we are handling hundreds of sharp knives, or maybe when we are testing an edge by shaving the face, we might get a little careless and cut ourselves. This cut was different, because it bled very profusely, but it also healed very quickly. The cut made by the extremely sharp edge bled much more profusely than the cut from the dull edge.

The same will hold true in the flesh of an animal, and since the arrow kills by causing the animal to bleed, then we obviously want our arrowheads to be just as sharp as possible. It could mean the difference between a deer that gets away and venison in the pot.

Most arrowheads have a good start as far as sharpness goes, but they all need help to some degree. Generally, the relief on an arrowhead is

Picture 7-1

pretty good, but the edge itself is questionable. If the edge is very smooth and sharp you only have to touch it up with a steel, but if it is rough or dull, you will have to restore it on the fine abrasive. If the arrow has been shot, check it very carefully for damage. Chances are it will have to be used for target practice from here on in. The shaft is probably in good shape, but the edge might be too far gone to bring it back to life. You must remember that you may get only one shot, and you have to count on that shot to down your game, so everything has to be perfect, especially the edge.

Sharpening an arrowhead is much like sharpening a knife blade, but you will use only the fine abrasive. Try to use the same angle as what the manufacturer originally ground in, as shown in Figure 7-8. If you use too little angle, you are

CROSS SECTION OF ARROWHEAD

Manufacturer's grind

Figure 7-8

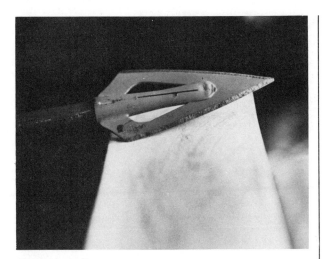

Picture 7-2

Picture 7-3

the stroke so that *all* of the edge will make contact with the abrasive. Use alternate strokes, and if there is any rust on the edge, you will have to do as many strokes as it takes to get rid of it. On most arrowheads, a few alternate strokes should be enough.

An alternate method that will be much easier and will give you a much better edge is using a guide like the one shown in Picture 7-4. A guide enables you to use a perfectly constant angle

Picture 7-4

forgiven, but if you use too much angle, you'll ruin your edge. Hold the arrow shaft in your hand, much like a knife handle, and start your stroke at the heel of the edge. Slowly draw the blade across the fine abrasive, making sure that the entire edge wipes it (Pictures 7-2 and 7-3). You will have to lift the shaft of the arrow through

and gives you complete control, and anytime you use a guide in sharpening, your edge will be much, much better than by hand. There is just no comparison.

When you get a good edge, touch it *lightly* on a smooth steel to give it that finishing touch (Pictures 7-5 to 7-8). It is also a good idea to touch the steel to the edge while you are waiting for your deer to show up. You are putting a lot of time and effort into that one critical shot, so everything should be one hundred percent perfect! As we said before, having the best possible edge on your arrowhead could mean the difference between the deer that got away, and venison steaks on the table. We wish you good hunting!

Picture 7-5

Picture 7-6

Picture 7-7

If the edge on your arrowhead feels rough, you will have to take it to the fine abrasive to do some grinding. If it feels very smooth you can just go to the steel, but always finish your arrowheads on a smooth steel.

In 7-5, Randy places the broadhead flat against the angle guide at the tip of the steel, and this gives him the proper angle. Now he "sets" his hand and wrist, and drops his arm, using the shoulder as the pivot point (7-6). As he reaches the bottom of the steel, he is all the way out on the tip of the blade (7-7). Two or three alternate strokes and you should be all set. If you are in the field, it would be much more convenient to use a pocket steel, as in 7-8.

Picture 7-8

The skinning knife seems to hold a certain fascination for most men, but there seems to be no such thing as a standard skinning knife. Most of the top professionals and sportsmen have their own idea of what this knife should look like and how it should work, so they design a blade that fits them. In our area there are trappers who go into the woods for weeks at a time and come out with pelts of mink, beaver, otter, muskrat, fox, and fisher. In skinning these critters, many trappers use a knife with a short, stubby blade. In the meat packing industry, where they are working on much larger animals, a typical skinning knife looks more like that in Figure 8-1. Try to picture a large steer hanging in front of a butcher. He reaches as high as he can to begin his cut on the leg, and then works his way down. You can see that regardless of the cutting position, the rounded blade will still be able to cut, whether the skinning surface is like that of A, B, or C. If this knife didn't have the long, rounded blade, but was cut off at the dotted line, skinning surface C would be just about impossible, and you would end up cutting through the hide. You can see in Figure 8-2 how you can reach out a considerable distance to begin a cut and pull it toward you, maintaining good edge contact throughout the cut.

In order to do a good job of skinning, you have to be accurate, so regardless of your blade design, the skinning knife must be extremely sharp to promote accuracy. Whether you are a butcher or a trapper, unnecessary cuts in the hide or pelt will mean money out of the pocket, so the edge on your knife is very, very important.

The knife we are using for this chapter (Picture 8-1) is one we made many years ago. The blade is made out of a piece of hacksaw blade, and although it doesn't look like it, the deer antler handle is quite comfortable. As always, the very first thing we do is check the relief of

CHAPTER 8

Sharpening the Skinning Knife

Figure 8-1

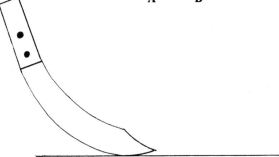

C

A   B

the blade (Picture 8-2). It will take some time and study to get used to feeling the relief, but this is very important, so keep at it.

Figure 8-3 shows a blade with a good relief, and a blade with a very poor relief. In A, notice how the thick relief at Points C and D is pushing the fingers apart even before the edge touches the skin. This would feel something like a piece of wire pushed between the fingers. Now look at B, where we have a very good relief. Here the cutting edge is first to touch the fingers, and the relief is so gradual that you will hardly feel your fingers being separated. This blade will sharpen very easily and will be excellent for skinning.

The knife we are going to sharpen is one that

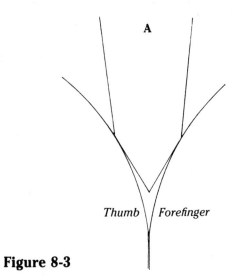

Figure 8-2

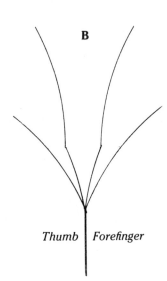

A

Thumb | Forefinger

B

Thumb | Forefinger

Figure 8-3

Picture 8-1

Picture 8-2

Picture 8-3

we have used in the past for some of our shaving promotions, so the relief happens to be excellent. We measured the relief angle and found it to be about 10°, which will sharpen very easily and very quickly. The trapper's skinning knife we showed you earlier has a very poor relief, and feeling the difference between the two will be a good way to get a better understanding of relief. In Picture 8-3 you can see the difference in the relief of the two blades.

When we place our blade on the coarse abrasive (Picture 8-4), we can feel the angle determined by the relief of the blade. We increase this angle just slightly to give clearance to the heel of the blade, and then begin scrubbing in

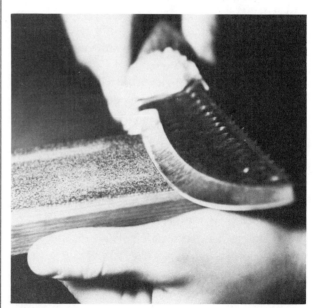

Picture 8-4

a good burr. Figure 8-4 will give you a better idea of what we are doing.

When the relief on a knife is as good as this one is, it will take only a few circular strokes on the coarse abrasive to turn up a good burr. Now

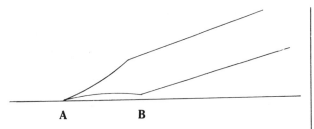

First we determine the relief angle by contacting the coarse abrasive at Points A and B, then we raise the back of the blade slightly, giving us clearance at Point B. Now we scrub in our burr.

Figure 8-4

we flip the blade over and scrub in a good strong burr on the other side. Again, after just a few strokes the burr pops up. A knife with a relief this good is just a pleasure to sharpen, and will also be a pleasure to use.

Now that we have run a burr on both sides of the blade, we are ready to go to the fine abrasive. Concentrate on picking up the hone as we taught you back in Chapter 2. Your index finger should be in the center of the hone and parallel to the sides (Picture 8-5). If you turn it over, the center of the hone should be over the ball of the thumb, which makes a good firm base. Before doing any grinding, make sure that all of your fingers are below the surface of the hone, so they don't get cut. Take your time and be satisfied with your grasp on the hone before proceeding. If you have any doubts, go back to Chapter 2 and refresh your memory on this subject.

Now place the blade on the fine hone near the handle, as in Picture 8-6. Increase the angle just a few degrees from what you used to grind in the burr on the coarse abrasive, and begin to draw the blade across the hone. As the blade travels across the hone, you will have to raise the handle, while

Picture 8-5

Picture 8-6

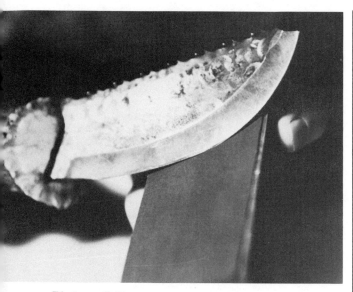

Picture 8-7

at the same time tilting your hone to aid in wiping the entire length of the edge across the abrasive (Picture 8-7). As you reach the end of the abrasive, you should be well up on the tip of the blade, as in Picture 8-8.

Most people prefer to stroke toward themselves to begin with, because it is easier to see what you are doing. You might like to use a mirror on the opposite stroke so you can watch your stroke and make sure your fingers are not in the way. When you have this mastered on both sides, use only alternate strokes. After about a dozen strokes, test the edge (Picture 8-9). Our edge feels perfect, and if you have done as well, the hide on that next skinning job will practically fall off the carcass!

Picture 8-8

Picture 8-9

CHAPTER 9
Sharpening the Ice Auger

If ever the sportsman lost his temper, it was with his ice auger. Even the most proper ice fishermen have a special vocabulary that they apply to their ice auger blades. You can usually tell who they are, because it looks as if they are going bald. (The result of pulling out hair while trying to sharpen this miserable tool.) Well, we're going to show you how to get your auger to bore ice better than when it was new. In fact, the thing will be so sharp the hair will probably grow back on our bald fishermen!

The ice auger is a fantastic invention and it would be difficult to give it enough praise. It wasn't that long ago when we had to hack our way through the ice with a chisel, but now we can effortlessly bore a hole through it in just a few minutes, provided that the blades are properly sharpened. If you live in an area like ours, where the ice can get over three feet thick, you can really appreciate this. It certainly makes ice fishing a lot more fun.

If you walk into a sporting goods store and check the price on a brand-new set of "sharp" auger blades, your heart will probably flutter a bit. The price of those things is unreal, and the sad part about it is that most fishermen don't even bother to try sharpening their old blades. They just take the path of least resistance and shell out their hard-earned cash for expensive new ones. Those dollars would do better to buy you some new fishing equipment (tell the wife it's for her), so watch closely as we show you how to sharpen your old blades and save your money.

Well, what is it that is so mind-boggling about this seemingly impossible-to-sharpen blade? *Nothing.* Just like everything else, if you understand this blade and its purpose, sharpening it is as easy as one, two, three; so let's study how the blade is made, why it is made that way, what goes wrong with it, and how we should fix it.

In Picture 9-1 are some typical auger blades with the typical grind. What kind of bevel do we have here? You got it—here again is the single bevel blade. Ideally these blades should be made of stainless steel because they get wet whenever you use them, but if they're not the manufacturer can sell a bunch of them to the fishermen who don't oil their blades and let them get rusty. After all, a rusty edge is a dull edge, and if you don't know how to sharpen this blade, you have no choice but to buy a new one.

In Figure 9-1 you can see how these blades are made. First a piece of steel is punched out to a basic blade design, as is indicated by the dotted lines. In forming the blade, both sides are actually ground to some extent, but we still consider this a single bevel blade. Line AB is what we call the drag side of the single bevel blade, as the material being cut passes over the top of it. Line BC is what we call the lead side of the edge. As you of course remember, we *never* touch an abrasive to the lead side of a single bevel unless it is flat against the side, and then only a fine abrasive. Many single bevel blades, such as plane blades, do not have side BC ground in on the lead side of the edge, so in honing this side on the auger blade you must keep the abrasive flat to side BC.

Well, what is it that goes haywire with these ice auger blades? As we said before, rust is one thing. You should always dry the blade and wipe a thin film of oil on it to preserve the edge from rust. Another thing is what we call "stomping." And what is this? If you watch some fishermen start their hole, you'll know what stomping is. It looks like they think they're still using an ice chisel, because they take their augers and stomp them onto the ice—as if this were going to help them get their hole started.

In Figure 9-2 you can see what effect this has on the blade. By slamming the auger on the ice,

Picture 9-1

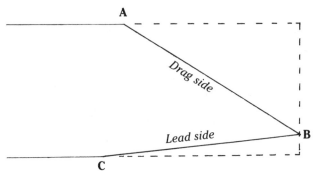

Figure 9-1

the edge is bent so the contact point is not the actual cutting edge, but the bend behind it. To remedy this situation and straighten the edge, we have to wipe it with a smooth steel at the

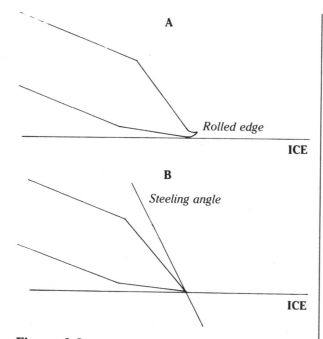

A

Rolled edge

ICE

B

Steeling angle

ICE

Figure 9-2

approximate angle shown in B. Use the weight of your hand and give each blade a few swipes (Picture 9-2).

When you are steeling, pay special attention to where the edge first contacts the ice. This is your "stomping area" and is probably the part of the blade that is causing you the trouble. After all, before you can drill a hole in the ice, you first have to get started, and if this first part of the edge has been turned up, you'll never get started!

When you have steeled the blades a few times, see how well the auger cuts the ice (Picture 9-3). If you feel no difference, try steeling a few more times, using a little more pressure, and

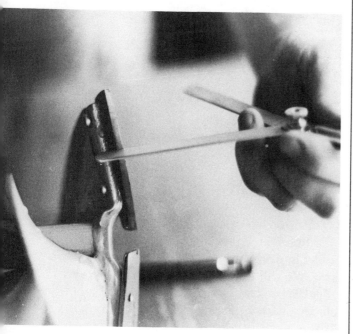

Picture 9-2

Picture 9-3

then try it again. At the last local fishing contest here on Shagawa Lake, we armed ourselves with only a steel and went around sharpening every auger in sight. Those fishermen couldn't believe the results, and you probably won't either. So don't be a stomper, but place your auger carefully on that hard ice.

If you have an auger that has been used, abused, or just improperly sharpened, the edge will probably be too far gone for just a steel to do any good. In this case you will have to remove the blades and completely resharpen them. In Figure 9-3 we have a blade on which someone has committed the cardinal sin of the single bevel—he ground metal from the lead side. Now the blade is riding over the ice on the heel in back of the actual cutting edge. To fix this situation we will have to grind side AB back until we have what looks like CD, so that the actual cutting edge will contact the ice instead of that rounded heel. Our hollow grinder would be perfect for this job, but we can also grind it by hand if we have to.

When we are finished with this job we will have a burr pointing downward from side CD, and from here we will finish the edge on a fine abrasive by hand. Throughout the sharpening process, it would be a good idea for you to study your progress in each step with a magnifying glass. The more you look, the more you will learn!

The first thing we will do now is get rid of that burr. We must remember that we have a single bevel blade here, so we have to make sure that the lead side is always flat to the abrasive (Picture 9-4). Stroke the entire edge now, until the burr has disappeared, always making sure that the lead side is flat to the abrasive. When the burr is gone, turn the blade over and stroke the other side at an angle slightly greater than you used to grind in that drag side. *Alternate* with

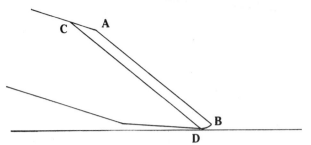

Figure 9-3

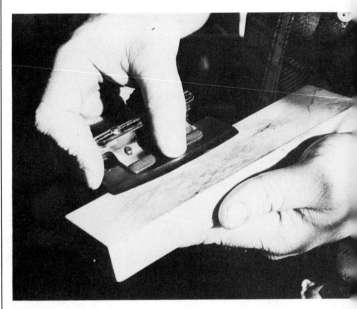

Picture 9-4

about a dozen strokes and then test the edge (Picture 9-5). If it is not quite good enough, try a few more alternate strokes on the fine abrasive. We will only accept an absolutely perfect edge! When your edge is perfect, replace the blades and try the auger on the ice.

Now we will improve the edge a little more, and maybe learn something in the process. *Lightly*

Picture 9-5

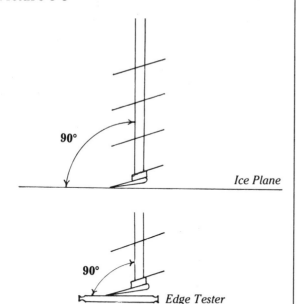

90°

Ice Plane

90°

Edge Tester

Figure 9-4

If the edge "bites" the test when contacted at the same angle as the ice plane, it will also cut ice very easily.

steel the bottom, or lead side, of the edge two or three times, and then the top, or drag side, a few times, using a little more pressure than you did on the bottom. This should turn the cutting edge down a bit, and into the ice. Try the auger again and it should be a little better yet.

If you don't want to bother with steeling the edge out on the ice, you can do it in the comfort of your home and still check the results. All you need is an Edge Tester like the one shown in Picture 9-5. The cutting edge must contact the ice properly in order to have good penetration, and we can determine this very simply with the Edge Tester. We just touch the Tester to the edge at the same angle that the ice would meet it. This will be in a position perpendicular to the shaft of the auger, as shown in Figure 9-4. Test the entire length of both blades (Picture 9-6) and especially the first inch or so, because this

Picture 9-6

is your "stomping" area. If the edge "bites" into the tester easily, you can be assured that it will also bite into the ice. If you find a weak spot, wipe it with the steel as we did earlier until you get the proper effect.

We tried our auger out on the ice after we sharpened it, and it cut the ice like a dream. When we exerted too much downward pressure, the edge bit the ice so hard we couldn't even turn it, but as we eased up on the pressure, it cut very nicely. In measuring our cutting, we found we could cut 3/4″ of ice per revolution. Now that's cutting ice!

Yes, the ice auger is a great tool, but just as with any other tool, we have to be concerned with *safety*. The auger can cause tragedy if not properly used. Some fishermen like to mix a few brews with their fishing, which always makes using a sharp tool more dangerous. One day one of the local fellows was out fishing and left his auger lying near his hole. When he got a strike, he ran over to reel his fish in, and in the confusion he cut the underside of his wrist. The nasty gash went all the way into his tendons, and ruined his fishing for a long, long time. Just

the thought of such a cut is enough to give you the willies, especially on such a vulnerable area as the wrist. This is just one of the many reasons we try to emphasize the importance of using slow, careful movements in both the sharpening and in the use of edged tools. So always remember that when you are finished with your auger, you should either drill it into the ice just enough to make it stand up, or put the blade guard in place.

You must also use extreme caution whenever you are removing or replacing the blades from the auger. If you don't use your head, one little slip of the wrench and you could ram your hand right across the sharp blade. Always make sure that your hand is positioned behind the cutting edge, so that if you happen to slip, your hand will fly away from the edge, instead of into it.

A little safety awareness might prevent you from someday spilling your precious red corpuscles onto the nice white snow—and ruining a good day of fishing.

CHAPTER 10
Sharpening Fishhooks

We have all heard about "the lunker that got away." It's a tale familiar to every sportsman who ever baited a hook. But have you ever stopped to wonder why there are so many "lunkers" that get away? When a fish strikes with such force it almost certainly has the bait in its mouth, right along with the hook. Something must be wrong here, so let's take a closer look.

As you already know, the inside of the mouth of a fish is rather hard, and it seems that the bigger the fish, the harder it is. Now the idea behind fishing is to catch fish, so you need a hook that will penetrate this hard surface inside the fish's mouth. If you are fishing with a dull hook, you are likely to go home with just a stringer full of fish stories.

Our study of fishhooks taught us that the same is true of a new hook as is true of any other brand-new edged tool: it must be sharpened before you can use it. The way to test whether a fishhook is sharp is to drag it across the surface of an Edge Tester, as shown in Picture 10-1. If the hook doesn't "bite" into the surface of the Edge Tester, but slides across it, you can bet that it won't bite into the tough, bony structure of the fish's mouth, either. The only way to remedy this is to sharpen the hook. You might not have as many tall tales to tell, but you will certainly have more fish in the frying pan.

Fishhooks have been around for many, many years, so you would think that the companies making them certainly must know what they're doing, right? Well, look at any new hook under a good magnifying glass, and you'll wonder why *all* the fish don't get away. This might come as a surprise, but most every fishhook you can buy will have a poor point on it. Just as with the knife manufacturer, a hook company might know how to build the best hook in the world, but that doesn't mean they know beans about edges.

In order to understand more clearly how a fishhook is made and how it should be sharpened, we are going to reproduce a fishhook point on a 3/8″ bridge spike. Even though this will be much larger than any fishhook you will ever use, it will be easier to see how a hook should be sharpened, and then we will apply the same principle to the standard fishhook.

Close study of a hook point shows that it is ground from three sides, and has one surface that has been untouched, as shown in Figure 10-1. You can see how the hook point has a long main grind and forms an edge on each side when it meets the two finish grinds. You will also see that the back side of the hook point is left intact, and that the very end of the point is usually bent slightly toward the stem of the hook. In Pictures 10-2 and 10-3 we are trying to duplicate these grinds on our 3/8″ spike.

Now the question is, do we sharpen the point on the outside edge, or on the inside edge toward the stem? To determine this, take a look at Figure 10-2. All we have to do is draw a line bisecting the edge angle, as is indicated by the dotted lines, and this will tell us in what direction the tip is pointing. As you can see, there is a big difference between A, where the outside edge was sharpened, and B, where the inside was sharpened. The hook point in A will have a tendency to ride across the surface of the fish's mouth, while the point in B will bite it, so you can set the rest of the hook firmly into that monster's mouth. It is quite obvious that we want to sharpen our hook like the one in B.

Figure 10-3 will give you a little better idea of what we are doing to the hook point. In A we have an average hook as it comes from the factory; in B a hook that we have sharpened. You can see that in sharpening the hook point, we are actually grinding off the old tip, and we end up with two additional surfaces. Don't be too

Picture 10-1

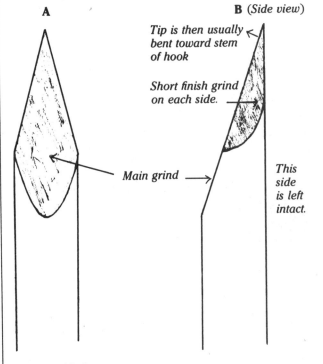

A

B (*Side view*)

Tip is then usually bent toward stem of hook

Short finish grind on each side.

Main grind

This side is left intact.

Figure 10-1

Picture 10-2

Picture 10-3

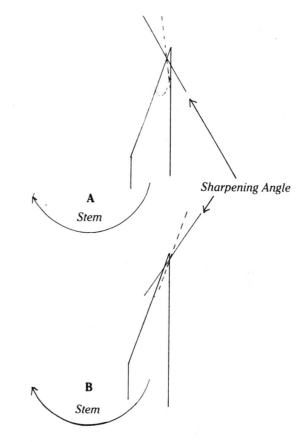

A

Stem

Sharpening Angle

B

Stem

Figure 10-2

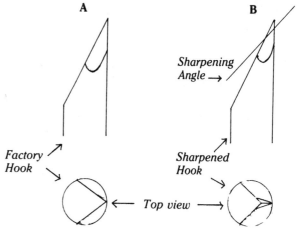

A

B

Sharpening Angle →

Factory Hook →

Sharpened Hook →

← *Top view* →

Figure 10-3

concerned with a precise sharpening angle, but use what works best for you. It is also going to take a little experimenting to get the hang of this. You might be a little confused right now, but the next pictures should clear it up for you.

Now we will put theory into practice and sharpen the hook point we have duplicated on the bridge spike. In Picture 10-4 you can see what the final point should look like. Now if we can put as good an edge on a fishhook as we have on this spike, we'll catch all kinds of fish!

Our next step is to put an identical, but much smaller, version of this point on a fishhook, but before we start let's see how well it works as it comes from the factory. First we drag it across a piece of paper, and in Picture 10-5 you can see that the hook refuses to bite it. When we checked it on a Tester we also got a zero.

Most hones are going to be too thick for this project, especially if you are going to sharpen small hooks, so it will be best to use a fine coated abrasive. Start with the largest hook you can find so that you can see and more clearly understand what you are doing. Place the hook on the abrasive as in Picture 10-6, and move the hook back and forth about a dozen times, trying to maintain a constant angle. Then turn the hook over, and do the same on the other side.

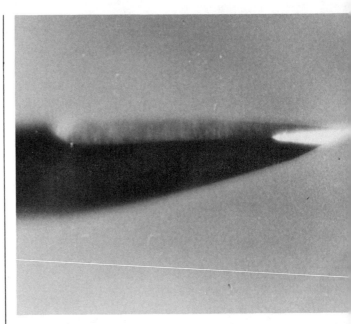

Picture 10-4

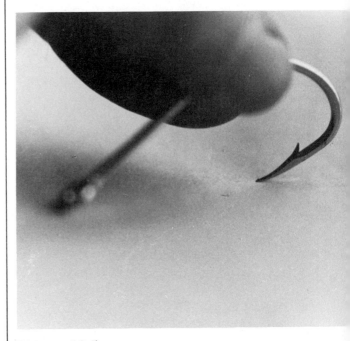

Picture 10-5

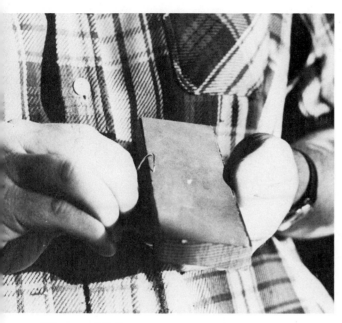

Picture 10-6

Now when we drag the hook over the paper it bites and penetrates very easily (Picture 10-7). Imagine what it will do now in that lunker's mouth when he tries to mess around with your bait!

We have found that a sharp fishhook is good for things other than fishing, too. On one fishing trip, one of us got a painful sliver well below the surface of the skin. Tweezers would have been useless even if we had had a pair. We had no pins, either, and were getting desperate, so we tried one of the fishhooks we had just sharpened. We probed into the wound and when the hook was pulled out, lo! ... the sliver was impaled on the tip of the hook! Well, little doubt there was a lot of luck in spearing that painful sliver, but there's no doubt either that the hook was very sharp.

You will probably goof a few times before getting good tips on your hooks, but don't let this bother you. Anything you do will be an improvement over what you have now. Be sure to test every hook before you use it, and before long you'll be very efficient with your hook sharpening, and a lot more successful in your fishing, too!

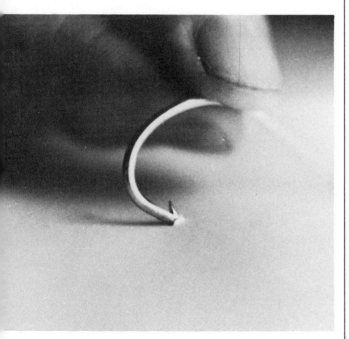

Picture 10-7

CHAPTER 11

Sharpening Scissors

One of the most common yet most misunderstood tools around is the scissors. It seems that most people do not understand how they work or how they should be sharpened. One man who sharpened scissors for a living told us that whenever someone brought in a pair of scissors that were to be used on doubleknits, he would break out in a cold sweat, so we decided to do some more testing with scissors. We had already had some experience sharpening scissors for the tanning industry, where they use many scissors in trimming operations. The scissors are much more accurate in trimming than a knife, and because leather is so expensive, accuracy in trimming is very important.

In studying scissors, we have found that, as with so many other tools, the problem is usually not with the scissors; the problem is understanding them. If they are sharpened properly they will work very well, but if they are dull you will come to despise them.

The cutting edge on our pair of scissors is not nearly as bad as many that we have seen, but they are very hard to close. Many times a scissors will be adjusted too tight to make up for a poor edge, and then the blades are not actually cutting, but are pinching the material apart. You can see the results of a dull pair of scissors through high magnification in Picture 11-1. Here you can see that in cutting paper, the dull scissors have left a very ragged, fuzzy cut. This paper has been pinched apart rather than cut. If the scissors were sharp, the cut would look very clean and clear.

All you have to remember is that a pair of scissors is just a single bevel blade, and so it should be sharpened just like any other single bevel blade. You can sharpen both blades, or if they are both in good shape, you can make them work well by sharpening only one blade.

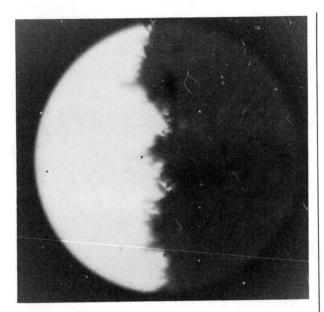

Picture 11-1

The first thing we have to do is improve the relief of the scissor blade we are going to sharpen. It's going to take a little grinding, so we will use our hollow grinder. It's always best to take the scissors apart when you sharpen them, so you will only be working with one blade, which will be much easier to handle. Unfortunately, many scissors are put together with a screw that has been knurled over so that it won't turn out. Sometimes we will just grind the knurled part of the screw down to where it will turn out.

If you do your grinding on the hollow grinder, you'll have to set up a wood block to use as a guide for the blade, as shown in Figure 11-1. Position the block so the right edges of both the block and the grinding wheel are about even; this will allow you to grind all the way to the hilt of the scissor blade, as in B. In A, notice the direction of rotation of the grinding wheel. Always make sure you place the block on the correct side of the wheel so your work is not drawn

into it. Use the *up* side of the wheel, and push your work away, which is much safer. Also, make sure you wear your safety glasses when using the grinding machine.

Before you start grinding, try to get the feel of what you will be doing with the motor turned off. Lay the scissor blade *flat* on the wood block so that the wheel contacts the edge of the blade.

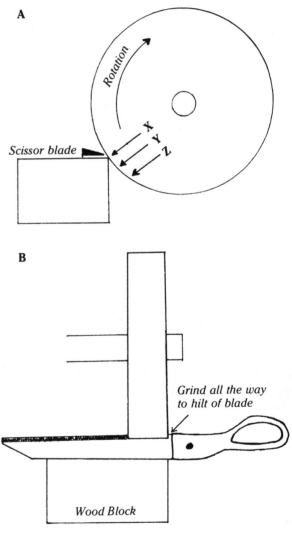

Figure 11-1

Start at the hilt of the blade, as in B, and draw the blade across the wheel, toward the tip of the blade. When you feel sure of what you are doing, you can turn the motor on.

Picture 11-2

Picture 11-3

Now we will take a "print" to see what kind of contact the grinding wheel is making with the blade (Picture 11-2). Our first print in Picture 11-3 shows that we need a little more angle. In A of Figure 11-1, you can see that if we want to increase the bevel, we have to move the wood block from position X to position Y or Z. The farther the block is moved toward the bottom of the wheel, the greater the bevel on the blade will be. When you get a satisfactory print (Picture 11-3) tighten the wood block down and you are ready to do your grinding.

Now lay the blade *flat* on the wood block so that it makes contact with the wheel as close to the back of the blade as possible (Picture 11-4).

Picture 11-4

If you were not able to take your scissors apart, you'll have to watch that the other blade doesn't get in the way of the wheel and ruin the edge. As you're moving the blade across the grinding wheel, rather than let your fingers get too close to it, use a small piece of wood to maintain blade contact with the wheel. The last thing you need is a ground-off fingernail! Slowly and lightly draw the blade across the wheel, and when the tip is even with the left side of the wheel, stop. If you pull it all the way out you will lose your geometry at the tip because the blade will no longer be flat on the base to give you control. It's better to angle the handle of the blade back, as shown in Figure 11-2, and grind the tip of the blade on the edge of the wheel. This way you can leave the blade flat on the guide block and maintain complete control.

It might seem you are doing an awful lot of grinding, but keep going until you have run a burr along the entire length of the edge. When you get a good burr, go to the fine abrasive and lay the blade *flat*, as shown in Picture 11-5. Start at the hilt of the blade, and draw it across the abrasive, making sure that the whole edge wipes it. Do this stroke six or eight times, using only the weight of your hand and arm, and this will remove the overhanging burr.

Now turn the blade over and use an angle slightly greater than what you ground in on the hollow grinder (Picture 11-6). If you use too little angle, the cutting edge will not contact the abrasive, and you will be able to see a dark shadow under the edge, as illustrated in Figure 11-3. Increase the angle just a little, until this shadow disappears, and then try to maintain this angle throughout the stroke. Remember to use slow, careful strokes so that you can study what you are doing. Try to maintain a constant angle, and make sure that the whole edge wipes the abrasive. Finish up with a few alternate strokes, and then test the edge (Picture 11-7). We found a bad spot in our edge, and with the magnifying glass we saw it was a rust spot, so we gave it a few more strokes on the fine abrasive. Now when we test it, it feels just about perfect.

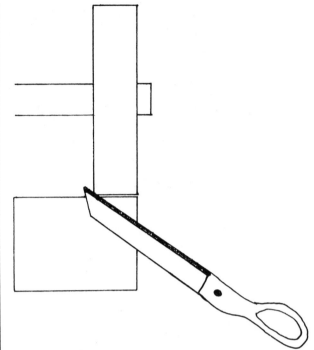

Figure 11-2

Picture 11-5

Picture 11-6

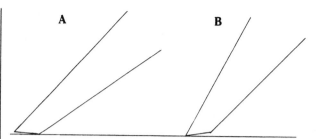

Figure 11-3

If you use too little angle, as in A, the cutting edge will not contact the abrasive and you will see a dark shadow under the edge. Increase the angle slightly until the shadow disappears, and then you will be up on the cutting edge, as in B.

Picture 11-7

Picture 11-8

We have one more important step before we use these scissors. What we want to make sure is that one blade will not cut into the other as they meet and pass by. To do this we will run a smooth steel across the flat side of the blade (Picture 11-8), using just a slight angle, as shown

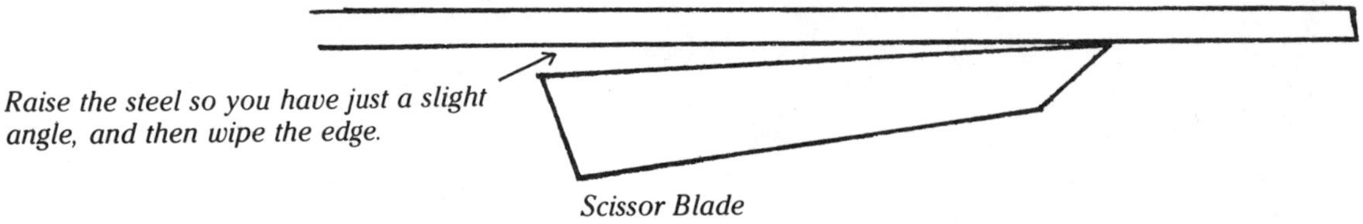

Raise the steel so you have just a slight angle, and then wipe the edge.

Scissor Blade

Figure 11-4

in Figure 11-4. This will point the cutting edge slightly away from the other blade, preventing them from destroying each other.

Now to see just how well our sharpened scissors will cut, we have folded a newspaper about sixty layers, and the scissors cut through it quite easily. When we look at the cut through the microscope, it looks very clear and clean, and you can compare the results of the scissors when they were dull, and then when they were sharpened, in Picture 11-9.

Now that you understand how a pair of scissors works and how they should be sharpened, you will have no more problems with them. A sharp pair of scissors will work well on just about anything, whether you are tying flies or cutting leather straps for your packsack.

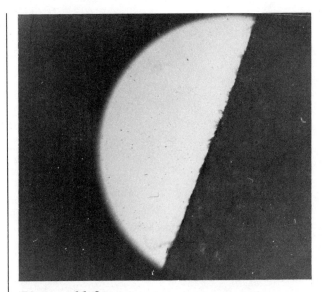

Picture 11-9

Now we are going to sharpen one of the sportsman's most popular knives, the sheath knife. The knife we are using is not an expensive one, but that doesn't really have anything to do with the results of sharpening. Some inexpensive knives are easier to sharpen than many of the more expensive ones, for the expensive ones often have poor relief. The blade on this knife is about 5 1/2″ long and about 1″ deep. It would make a rather good knife for the hunter because it's plenty big and yet it's nice and light. The handle has a guard at both ends, which also makes it a safe-to-use knife.

As always, the first thing we do is check the relief of the blade. This one isn't all that bad, but we will improve it, of course. Because we have quite a bit of metal to remove, we will use a coarse hone rather than the coated abrasive. If we were just edging the knife and didn't have to remove much metal, the coated abrasive would work just fine.

Lay the blade almost flat on the coarse hone and begin grinding until the furrow marks extend all the way down to the edge. The nice, shiny finish comes off, but we make up for the lack of pretty shine in the sharpness department. And this reminds us of something. If you want to polish the blade on your knife, *don't* ever use a rag wheel to do it. These can be extremely dangerous on knives because they can grab either the edge or the tip and throw it with great speed. You or someone in the area could be seriously hurt. This is one of the hazards of custom knife-making, and many superb craftsmen have been seriously hurt while polishing a blade. So the word is *don't!*

Although this knife isn't that bad, most knives come from the factory with a very poor relief. What we want to do is grind off all the excess metal so that the relief will end up looking some-

CHAPTER 12

Sharpening the Sheath Knife

thing like the dotted lines in Figure 12-1. When you have both sides ground, check your relief, and when you are satisfied with it you are ready to do your sharpening.

We are going to use a sharpening guide on this knife, and in Picture 12-2 you can see that we have mounted the guide as far back as possible on the blade. This will give us a good secondary edge face angle, and when we measure it (Picture 12-2), we find we have an angle of about 35°. Now don't get thrown by that big number, because our actual grinding angle to the hone will be only half of that, or about 17° or 18°.

With the guide firmly clamped in place, we go to the coarse hone to begin grinding in the secondary edge face. Always remember to touch the guide to the hone first, and then the edge. This will prevent you from ruining the edge, and it is even more critical when you are finishing the edge on the fine abrasive. Now continue grinding until you get that all-important burr running the entire length of the edge, and then flip it over and do the same thing for the other side. When you have run a good burr on both sides, you are ready to go to the fine abrasive for finishing (Picture 12-3).

Now we have to increase the grinding angle slightly to give us our double-edging effect. To do this, we reposition the sharpening guide about 1/8" *toward* the edge and 1/8" *toward* the tip of the blade. As you can see in Figure 12-2, just the very tip of the edge will be contacting the abrasive, and the edge will set very quickly.

We now place the guide on the abrasive *first,* and then the edge. If we were to touch the edge to the abrasive first, we could "roll" the edge and ruin it. Start at the heel of the blade, as shown in Picture 12-4, and slowly draw the blade across the abrasive. As you draw the blade across, carefully study the contact between the edge

When we took this knife out of the package we found a caution sign, warning us to use care with the sharp knife. This made us curious, so we checked it with our Edge Tester, and on a scale of 100 we found it to be about 50. For a factory edge this is pretty good, and although it's better than most it still needs a lot of help.

Picture 12-1

Figure 12-1

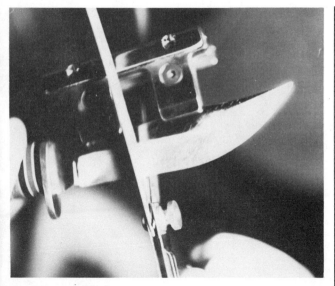

Picture 12-2

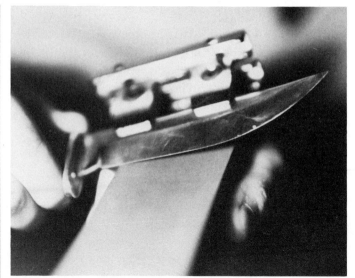

Picture 12-4

Picture 12-3

The position of the blade in A is what we used on the coarse hone to grind in the secondary edge faces. Then when we go to the fine abrasive, we increase the angle just enough to give the heel of the secondary edge face a slight clearance, as in B. Now the primary edge will "set" very quickly because there is an extremely small area of the blade contacting the fine abrasive. This is what we call double-edging.

Figure 12-2

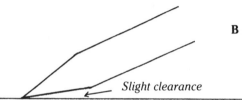

A

B

Slight clearance

and the abrasive, making sure that the whole edge gets wiped. At the midpoint of the stroke you should be at about the center of the blade (Picture 12-5), and as you reach the end of the abrasive you should be up on the tip of the blade (Picture 12-6). Remember, the most used and therefore most important part of the blade is the first two inches or so, back from the tip, so make sure your contact is good in this area.

When you have practiced this finishing stroke on both sides, use only alternating strokes. Concentrate on making your stroke smooth and even,

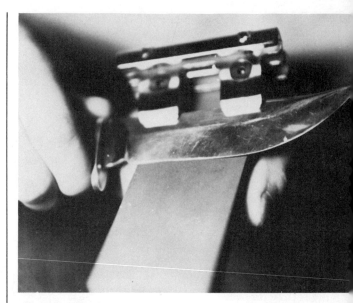

Picture 12-5

Picture 12-6

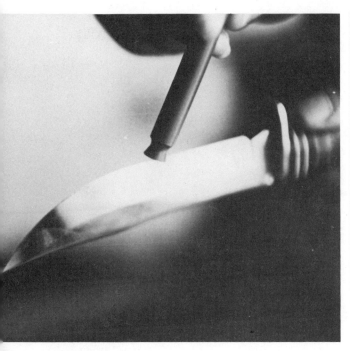

Picture 12-7

and don't make the common mistake of hurrying off the abrasive at the end of the stroke—this will foul up the edge. After about a dozen strokes, test your edge to see what you have (Picture 12-7). If your edge doesn't feel perfect, give it a few more *very light* strokes on the fine abrasive, and then test it again. This did the trick on our knife, and now it feels perfect. Joe, one of our boys, used this knife to clean out his deer and said it was "excellent," but his inexperienced partner said, "It's too sharp!"

The chain saw. Mere mention of that name will get you many reactions. It's complex, misunderstood, dangerous, even frightening. If mishandled, the chain saw can produce a wound that is terrible beyond description. Most edges, like a knife or ax, will simply part the flesh, and the wound can be stitched or even taped shut. But not the chain saw. When it cuts, it will gouge out a devastating wound. Yes, the chain saw commands tremendous respect. As people try to become more self-sufficient, the chain saw is gaining in popularity, and with good reason—it is a tremendous work saver. Because it is so popular, and so potentially dangerous, we will certainly stress chain saw safety.

Just like all other edged tools, the chain saw is much more dangerous when it is dull than when it is sharp. When your saw becomes dull, you have to start fighting it, and you have to bear down in order to make it cut. After a few minutes of this you start to become tired and careless—an open invitation for an accident. The only problem is that for most people sharpening the chain saw is a mystery. Well, what is so difficult about sharpening the chain saw? If we understand the tool, nothing is difficult about it, so let's take a closer look.

Before we even concern ourselves with sharpening, there are some other things we have to be concerned with that also affect the cutting ability of the tool. Many times these saws suffer from improper lubrication; and a badly worn chain or bar can really give you fits. Everybody just seems to be worried about how the saw cuts rather than proper lubrication. In Figure 13-1 you can see what effect a worn bar will have in cutting. This is a cross section of a bar, and the chain runs in the groove. When the bar is in good shape, the tops are square so that the cutting teeth will be held straight. If you don't

CHAPTER 13
Sharpening the Chain Saw

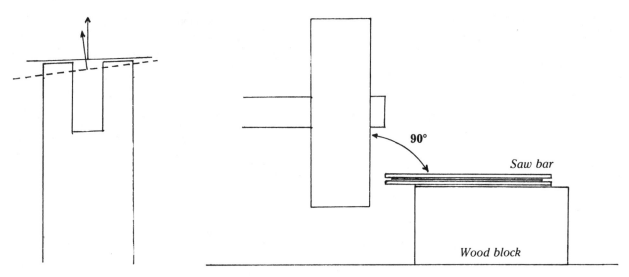

Figure 13-1   **Figure 13-2**

believe in using oil, pretty soon the bar will become worn, as is indicated by the dotted lines. Now the teeth are headed off in another direction, as shown by the arrow, and as you get deeper into your cut, the more trouble you will have. To remedy this situation, remove the bar and take it to the grinding wheel, as shown in Figure 13-2. Just make sure that the bar is 90° to the edge of the grinding wheel, and then square off the tops of the grooves. When you are finished, make sure the groove is clean of all the grit and chips, and then you are back in business. Now make sure that the chain is getting proper lubrication, and this problem won't be back to haunt you for quite a while.

The next thing we should check is the tension of the chain (Picture 13-1). Check the manufacturer's instructions and adjust the chain accordingly; this will help in cutting and also help in holding the teeth in place while they are sharpened.

Now we can get into sharpening the chain saw. It's very handy to clamp the bar of the saw

Picture 13-1

in a vise for sharpening, but that is not always practical. If you are working out in the woods and the saw goes dull, you'll have to sharpen without a vise, so it's best to get used to doing your sharpening without one.

In examining your chain saw, you will see we have our old friend, the single bevel blade. However, we have many single bevel blades, because a chain saw has many teeth, and each one has to be sharpened. You'll also notice something else between the teeth that is a big mystery to many people (Picture 13-2). These are called rakers, giving the impression that their main function is raking chips out of the cut. Actually, we prefer to call them gauges, because of the importance they play in limiting the depth of the

be about .02 inches. If we file the raker down, the depth of the chip plane, or cut, would increase, and if we file the raker down too far we could choke the saw because it would be trying to remove more chip than it is capable of handling. You will also notice that the raker is slightly tapered in the direction of travel, which will prevent it from "hanging up" on rough surfaces. To check your raker clearance, just place a straight edge across the top of two teeth, and measure it. To start with, use the clearance suggested by the manufacturer, and later do some experimenting if you wish. Don't be too concerned with an exact measurement in the thousandths. With a little experience you'll be able to eyeball it and get good results.

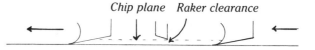

Figure 13-3

Picture 13-2

cut, as you can see in Figure 13-3. Notice the difference in height between the top of the teeth and the top of the raker. This would probably

To understand better how the rakers work, we could compare them to the wood plane. A plane blade is mounted on a base, and then extends out the bottom of the base to contact the wood, as shown in Figure 13-4. The farther out the blade extends, the deeper the cut will be, and if you go too far you won't even be able to push the plane because it will be cutting too deeply into the wood. So in other words, the base is what limits the depth of the cut, and without the base there would be no control. Well, the raker on the chain saw works the same way.

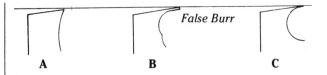

Figure 13-5

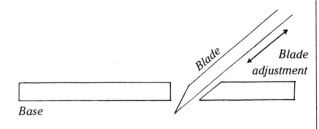

The base limits the depth of cut on the plane, just as the raker limits the depth of cut on the chain saw.

Figure 13-4

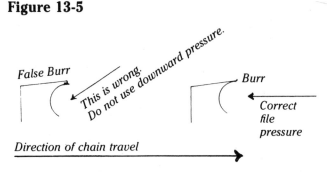

Figure 13-6

There is a raker on each side of the tooth and they limit the depth of the cut. The only difference is that the plane blade is adjustable, whereas the rakers on the chain saw all have to be filed down to the proper depth cut.

In sharpening the teeth, make sure your file is the right diameter. As you can see in Figure 13-5, if your file is either too big or too small it will not sharpen properly. In A, someone used a file that was too big, and the result is a very blunt edge. The tooth will also wear out very quickly if the file is too large. The tooth in B was filed with too small a file, and you can see that the two edge faces do not meet to form an edge. It's even possible to file a "false burr" and be fooled into believing you have done a good job. A false burr is one that occurs somewhere other than on the side opposite the one you are grinding. In this case it's on the face of the dull edge and would be very hard to see with the naked eye. The tooth in C has been sharpened with the proper diameter file, and you can see that the two edges meet to form a burr.

In filing your chain saw, don't get all shook up about using an exact angle, because it's not that important for general use. The factory-ground angle should work well for you. We usually like to sharpen with the file about 65° to the bar. If we were going to be ripping logs, rather than cross cutting, we would be better off sharpening at an angle greater than 65°.

While sharpening your chain, make sure that you use pressure *only* straight toward the back of the tooth, as shown in Figure 13-6. This way the two edge faces are certain to meet and form a good burr. If you use downward pressure, you will be working away from the cutting edge, and might be fooled by feeling a false burr.

You must also remember to apply pressure only when you are *pushing* the file, as in Figure 13-7, and never when you are pulling it back. This is because the file is constructed with the

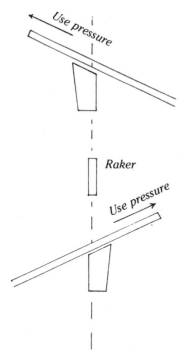

Figure 13-7

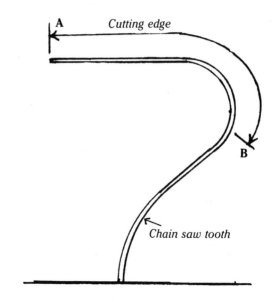

The cutting edge includes the curved part of the tooth, so you must run a burr from point A to point B.

Figure 13-8

lay of teeth pointing toward the tip, so it will only cut in this direction. You can compare this to the handsaw. It cuts only when you push it because of the lay of the teeth. If you apply pressure when you pull the saw back, you will only make it dull, and the same is true of the chain saw file. So only apply pressure when you are pushing it and it will last longer.

File each tooth until you can feel a good burr all along the cutting edge, as shown in Figure 13-8. The actual cutting edge on the tooth includes part of the curve, so you must run a burr all the way from point A to point B. When you get one tooth finished, continue all the way around the chain until each tooth has been sharpened. Some folks like to sharpen all the way around on one side (Picture 13-3), and then finish the

Picture 13-3

other, while others prefer to alternate to each tooth (Picture 13-4). It doesn't matter how you do it, just so you get a good burr on every tooth. Although you should be able to tell where you started, you might like to mark the first tooth you sharpen so you know when you have gone all the way around the chain. You will probably find that you have a good side and an awkward side, but it is important that both sides get sharp, so take your time and do a good job.

When you move the chain, grab it on the top and bottom of the bar, and *pull it in the normal direction of travel* (Picture 13-5). The reason for this is that if you slip, your hand will not run into the sharpened edge of the teeth, but the dull back side. Some people like to wear gloves while sharpening for even greater protection. This might be a good idea, at least until you become more familiar with sharpening your chain saw.

Sharpening the chain saw is quite a bit different from sharpening most other tools, because it's one of the few cutting edges on which you can use a coarse abrasive only and get results that a professional would accept. You can even commit another sin of sharpening and get away with it, and that is leaving the burr on each tooth. This creates no problem because the burr doesn't stay there very long.

When you have finished sharpening each tooth and have checked the height of the rakers, go out and try your saw. If you have done a good job, it should now be a pleasure to use.

But don't forget about safety. First of all, *never* cut above your shoulders, because if you unexpectedly go through the branch, you will come down with the running saw on your legs. Always keep a stiff top arm, and this will prevent the saw from kicking back at you if the tip of the blade should grab something. Whenever you have to set your chain saw down, turn it off. A running

Picture 13-4

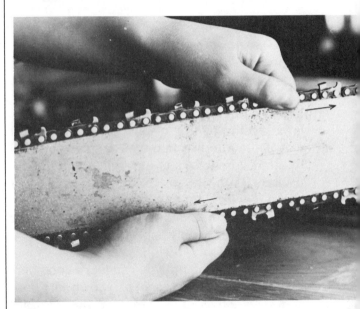

Picture 13-5

chain saw can be dangerous if you fall on it or bump into it. These saws throw a lot of chips all over, so always wear safety glasses, and if you are working out in the woods felling trees, put on a safety helmet. Many a logger has met his Waterloo when struck on the head by falling branches or trees. Read the manufacturer's safety instructions, and make sure the chain is properly lubricated. Last, but far from least, keep your saw sharp. A dull saw will cause you to become aggressive and fatigued, setting the stage for an accident. It's a sharp chain saw that makes for a safer chain saw.

Some Dos and Don'ts in Using a Chain Saw

The chain saw is such a "mean machine" that you have to treat it with tremendous respect. This is one edged tool that you never want to make that first mistake with, because it could be your last.

Picture 13-7

Picture 13-6 Don't *cut with just the tip of the saw. The chain could grab the log you are cutting and throw the saw up into your face. Instead you should cut with your chain saw in the position shown in Picture 13-7. Also keep a stiff upper arm to prevent any kickback. And do you see the end of that logging chain dangling over the wood pile? The other end has to be somewhere in that snow, so Randy better find it and remove the chain. Hitting steel is rough on a chain saw. It could dull your saw, and it could pull the teeth off and ruin the entire chain.*

Picture 13-8 *Cutting high adds to the danger of using a chain saw, so you must use extreme caution. Always make sure that your legs and feet are out of the path of travel when the chain saw cuts all the way through the log; or you could end up cutting into your own size 10's (Pictures 13-9 and 13-10).*

Picture 13-9

Picture 13-10

Picture 13-12

Picture 13-11 *Note how Randy is standing with his feet apart and has a stiff upper arm. This is a safer way to cut, and now when the chain saw drops through the log it will fall harmlessly between the feet. Also, keep the area around your feet clear, so that you don't stumble.*

Picture 13-12 Don't *ever cut above your shoulders. It's mighty dangerous. Randy also has his upper arm bent, and it would be very easy for this saw to jump back into his face. In Picture 13-13 you can see that if he drops the saw when he cuts through the branch, it will land right on his leg. That's a no-no.*

Picture 13-13

Picture 13-14 *This is a common mistake in using the chain saw. Many times, especially in limbing, your feet are blocked from your view, and you are not aware they are very close to the cutting chain. It would be quite easy to cut into your foot, so always make sure your feet are well out of the way.*

Picture 13-15 *If you have to set your saw down for some reason, and don't want to bother shutting it off, snub the chain by cutting into a log. This will prevent you from falling on or tripping over a moving chain, which could spell disaster.*

By no means does this completely cover chain saw safety, so read your manufacturer's safety instructions *carefully* and be sure to adopt safe operating practices right from the beginning. You should also use safety glasses and any other available safety equipment.

Always wear safety glasses when doing power cutting or grinding, or you risk having a chip fly into your eye and doing extensive damage.

Picture 13-16 *Here you can see what all this caution is about. The chain saw cuts a path about 5/16" wide. If you stop to think what this could mean in your leg or skull, you can't help but have all kinds of respect for the chain saw.*

One of the oldest tools around is the adz. Many years ago, the pioneers depended on this tool to form their logs and lumber in building their settlements. With all the modern tools and machinery today, the adz is almost forgotten, but you can still find some old-timers and back-to-nature folks using them. For those of you who are not familiar with this tool, you simply straddle the log you are working on and swing the adz between your legs, cutting a flat surface into the top of the log (Picture 14-1).

We picked up an old adz from one of the local junk shops to use for this demonstration. It is quite dull, and looks as though someone has used it as a hoe. When we tried it out on a piece of aspen, the results were very poor. It didn't cut the wood, but just tore it off, leaving a rough, ragged cut. Obviously, this adz needed a lot of help.

What kind of edge do we have on the adz? The single bevel blade again. And the main thing to remember about the single bevel blade is that we never touch an abrasive to the flat side of the edge, unless it is perfectly flat against that side, and then *only* with a fine abrasive. Generally, the side we *do not* grind is the side facing the material to be cut, which we refer to as the lead side.

In Figure 14-1 we have a drawing of our adz blade, and it's easy to see why it doesn't cut. Someone has either improperly sharpened it or has abused it, and the edge has taken a rounded shape. No matter how it happened, we'll have to do major surgery to get it back into shape. It's going to take a lot of grinding, but we have to get rid of that rounded edge, so we have to grind the drag side down to the dotted line, as in Figure 14-1. Remember, the lead side is what faces the log, and the drag side is what faces the chips, so we have to make sure the lead side

CHAPTER 14
Sharpening the Adz

Picture 14-1

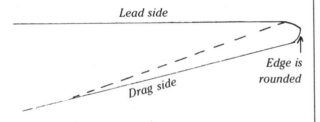

Lead side

Edge is rounded

Drag side

Figure 14-1

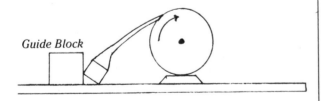

Guide Block

Figure 14-2

is turned up from the abrasive when we do our grinding.

To make this sharpening job much easier, we will take the handle off and go to the hollow grinder to improve the relief and grind out all the nicks from the edge. We will have to set up a guide on the hollow grinder, much the same way we did when we sharpened the ax, as in Figure 14-2. First we will take a print to see how the grinding wheel is contacting the blade (Picture 14-2). In Picture 14-3 you can see that the grind is a little too far from the edge, so we have to move the guide block a little farther *away* from the wheel. This time the print looks pretty good, so we can begin our grinding.

We must continue grinding until the two edges meet, forming a burr. In single bevel blades, we must always get a good strong continuous burr to make sure that the two edge faces meet. In Picture 14-4 you can see that we still have a ways to go, although the grind is starting to look pretty good. After a little more grinding, we now have a good strong burr running the entire length of the edge, and the relief of the blade is looking pretty good. This is the proper way to feel for a burr (Picture 14-5).

Because this blade has been so beat up, we are going to have to grind the lead side a little bit to remove some rough and rust spots from the edge (Picture 14-6). Remember, we must keep the lead side flat to the abrasive, and it might not appear that we are doing so in the picture, but remember that the blade is curved. Now we will do a little more grinding on the drag side to make sure that we have a good strong burr running the entire length of the edge, and then we will be ready to do our sharpening.

When you go to the fine abrasive, it's always best to have the burr turned downward so that it will be removed. So take a few strokes across the fine abrasive on the lead side (Picture 14-

Picture 14-2

Picture 14-3

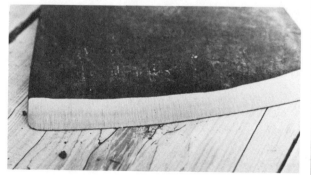

Picture 14-4

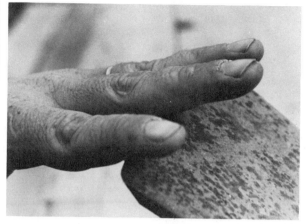

Picture 14-5

Picture 14-6

7), and then a few strokes on the drag side (Picture 14-8). We have to stay flat on the lead side, and use just enough angle on the drag side to give the hollow grind clearance. You'll be able to tell whether you're using enough angle by the fact that there is no dark shadow under the cutting edge (Picture 14-9). This indicates that the cutting edge is making good contact with the abrasive.

Now do about a dozen alternate strokes, and then test the edge (Picture 14-10). Our test tells

Picture 14-7

Picture 14-8

Picture 14-9

us that we evidently have some kind of problem, because we do not have a smooth edge. A look with the magnifying glass and we find a spot where the drag side does not meet the lead side (Picture 14-11). It was so small that it couldn't be seen with the naked eye, but this is the problem for sure. We will have to go back to the hollow grinder to do a little more grinding until we are sure the problem is taken care of.

Now we go back to the fine abrasive and do another dozen alternate strokes. This time when we test the edge it feels very good, except for one little rough spot at one end. We're going to leave it there, though, and see what, if any, effect it has in our cutting.

We try the adz out now, and wow, what a difference! The cut is very smooth, and notice the paper-thin chips we can cut (Picture 14-12). This is certainly indication of an excellent edge.

Picture 14-10

Picture 14-11

Picture 14-12

Picture 14-13

Picture 14-14

In Picture 14-13 you can see the result of the flaw we left in the blade. Do you see the wood fibers lying across the edge? The reason for this is that the edge was not sharp enough to cut them, so it just pulled them apart and they hung up on the imperfections in the edge. Whenever you see fibers lying over the cutting edge, you know that the edge could use some help.

Many times a second sharpening will take care of any flaws in the edge that the first sharpening didn't get. It could be a small nick or rust pit, and if you just start all over from scratch chances are that the flaw will disappear.

Just for the heck of it, we measured our final edge angle (Picture 14-14) to see what we ended up with, and found it to be about 25°. Now that you have a good edge on your adz, tell Mom and Junior no more digging stumps or potatoes with it!

CONCLUSION

WATCH FOR OUR NEXT BOOK

This is just the first of a series of books we are writing, and we hope that it has been helpful as well as enjoyable. There are still many things we have learned about the edge that we have not covered yet, so if you have questions or would like to learn more, we encourage you to watch for our future books. If we were to try putting everything we have learned about the edge and related subjects into one book, we would probably never finish it. Our future books will cover such things as sharpening the hobbyist's tools, sharpening farm machinery and tools, tips for using and choosing knives, sharpening tools for competition, and studying the edge under the microscope.

We will also be defining the edge. Have you ever stopped to think about what an edge is? If someone asked you to define an edge, what would you say? You might say that it is sharp, but what do you mean by sharp? What does a sharp knife have that a dull one doesn't? Now you've got something to think about. Ask someone else what an edge is, and you probably won't get a very clear answer. As important as the edge is, it seems that no one can define it. Well, we have done some work on this, and in one of our books we will try to define the edge for you.

We thank you for taking time to read this book, and if you have gone through it carefully you should be able to tackle just about any sharpening job. Remember, in everything you do, always be safe, and be the sharpest!

SHARE YOUR TIPS WITH US

In the many years we have been studying the edge, we have run into a lot of tips that we think you would be interested in. And for every one we have discovered, we have learned another from the people and professionals we have worked with. We would like to share these tips with you in one of our next books.

We would also like to hear from you. If you have some favorite tips and ideas concerning the use, care, sharpening, safety, dos, don'ts, etc., of any edged tools, we would really appreciate hearing about them. Or perhaps you have experienced an unusual accident with an edged tool that you can share with us to prevent someone else from making the same mistake.

If you would like to get on our mailing list to be notified when our new books are published, just send us your name and address. Also, if you have any suggestions, experiences, ideas, comments, or anything else you think might be helpful to us, we would be interested in hearing from you. If you still have questions about sharpening, though, we must ask you to be patient, and perhaps they will be answered in our next book. We get so many letters from people asking questions that we simply cannot answer them all. However, we are always looking for new ideas and will appreciate hearing about any experiences or suggestions you have.

Any tip that is submitted will be considered as granting us permission to use in publication, and if we use your tip we will send you the book in which it is used in addition to any similar books we write in the future.

We thank you in advance and look forward to hearing from you.

The products used in this book are available at your local hardware or sporting goods store or can be ordered from Razor Edge Systems, Inc. All correspondence should be directed to:

John Juranitch
c/o Razor Edge Systems, Inc.
P.O. Box 150
Ely, MN 55731

A FINAL THOUGHT

We have saved the most important topic for last so perhaps it will stick with you. So far in this book we have carefully covered all aspects of sharpening, from theory to actually grinding edges, and now you can probably put an incredible edge on most any tool. But now we are going to talk a little about something that is far more important than any of our tools.

In the world we live in, it's very easy to feel encumbered by life's demands and pressures. Sometimes we work so hard for our family, that pretty soon the family starts to become less important than the work. Or maybe we feel as if there are problems and pressures coming from all directions, or that we're just living to survive.

If you are feeling any of these things you're probably not getting much enjoyment out of living, and you might feel like your life has gone dull.

Well, there is Someone who wants to be a part of your life so that He can help you cope. He is God, our Creator. After all, we are the product of His workmanship, and He is concerned about quality, too. He didn't create us to live a life of worry, depression, or boredom. If you are feeling a bit insecure, or are troubled or perplexed and looking for answers, we invite you to look to God, for He loves you.

Your first step should be to find a good church and begin reading your Bible. Then as you allow Him to become a part of your life, you will find that it is a great blessing to have this security in these troubled times, and you will notice that He just sort of "sharpens" your life up for you!

AROUND THE HOME AND GARDEN

__THE ART OF FLOWER ARRANGING__ (M37-945, $8.95, U.S.A.)
by Zibby Tozer (M37-946, $11.50, Canada)

Flowers transform your home with their beauty, color, and fragrance. But how do you artfully arrange a single bloom or a mass of branches to achieve the perfect effect? Learn to create special moods in every room in styles ranging from modern to traditional. With the use of this special book and your own imagination, you will be able to add that special touch of joy and loveliness to your home.

Available in large-size quality paperback.

__THE COMPLETE BOOK OF GARDENING__
edited by Michael Wright (M38-045, $14.95, U.S.A.)
(M38-046, $17.95, Canada)

For every green thumb, budding or experienced, who wants to create a beautiful and exciting yet economical and easily managed garden, here is the encyclopedia extraordinaire of horticulture, with nearly 1,000 photos and illustrations—nearly 600 in full color. Covered in detail is every facet of planning, designing, constructing, and maintaining every type of outdoor garden.

Available in large-size quality paperback.

__THE RAZOR EDGE BOOK OF SHARPENING__
by John Juranitch (M38-002, $12.50, U.S.A.)
(M38-003, $13.50, Canada)

This book shows even the lowest-ranked beginner how to put the sharpest edge on the dullest blade and restore old knives and tools for years of trouble-free service and wear. Learn about the basic theory of sharpening, safe knife handling and use, sharpening the most popular blades in use today, and much, much more. This invaluable and readable book provides step-by-step lessons featuring over 100 photographs and drawings for ease and accuracy.

Available in large-size quality paperback.

WARNER BOOKS
P.O. Box 690
New York, N.Y. 10019

Please send me the books I have checked. I enclose a check or money order (not cash), plus 50¢ per order and 50¢ per copy to cover postage and handling.* (Allow 4 weeks for delivery.)

_____ Please send me your free mail order catalog. (If ordering only the catalog, include a large self-addressed, stamped envelope.)

Name _____

Address _____

City _____

State _____ Zip _____
*N.Y. State and California residents add applicable sales tax.   128

By the year 2000, 2 out of 3 Americans could be illiterate.

It's true.

Today, 75 million adults… about one American in three, can't read adequately. And by the year 2000, U.S. News & World Report envisions an America with a literacy rate of only 30%.

Before that America comes to be, you can stop it… by joining the fight against illiteracy today.

Call the Coalition for Literacy at toll-free **1-800-228-8813** and volunteer.

Volunteer Against Illiteracy. The only degree you need is a degree of caring.

Ad Council Coalition for Literacy

Warner Books is proud to be an active supporter of the Coalition for Literacy.